The Age of
German Liberation, 1795-1815

Friedrich Meinecke

The Age of
German Liberation, 1795–1815

Edited with an Introduction by PETER PARET

UNIVERSITY OF CALIFORNIA PRESS

Berkeley • Los Angeles • London

Translated by Peter Paret and Helmuth Fischer
from the sixth edition of
Das Zeitalter der Deutschen Erhebung
by Friedrich Meinecke, Vandenhoeck & Ruprecht, Göttingen,
1957, with permission.

University of California Press
Berkeley and Los Angeles, California

University of California Press, Ltd.
London, England

ISBN 0-520-03454-6
Library of Congress Catalog Card Number: 74-79767
Printed in the United States of America

2 3 4 5 6 7 8 9

Contents

Editor's Note

This translation is based on the sixth German edition, which varies only in a few details from the original text, published in 1906. In the first edition a different running head on each recto page identified major topics without interrupting the text as subheadings would have done. I have not followed this practice, rarely employed in American and English books today, but hope that the reader will find the addition of a chronology and of some footnotes helpful.

I am indebted to a number of friends and colleagues for their comments on my Introduction. Above all, I am deeply grateful to Felix Gilbert, whose observations preserved me from some, though surely not all, errors in discussing Meinecke's method and intellectual style. It is also a pleasure to thank Hans Herzfeld, Jeffrey Diefendorf, Charles McClelland, and my Stanford colleagues Gordon Craig, Lewis Spitz, and Hugh West, as well as Max Knight and William J. McClung of the University of California Press, for their interest and help.

Peter Paret

Stanford
July 1976

Friedrich Meinecke's Interpretation of the Age of German Liberation

BY PETER PARET

Friedrich Meinecke's *Age of German Liberation* is one of relatively few works in the literature to focus directly and exclusively on German history from the French Revolution to Waterloo. Far more common are books that discuss these years as part of a longer sequence or analyze them through the lives of significant contemporaries. Despite their titles, such classic interpretations as Ranke's *Hardenberg,* Lehmann's *Scharnhorst,* or Ritter's *Stein* are general histories; but they are organized around a man, not the period. Even Meinecke, some years before he published *Das Zeitalter der deutschen Erhebung,* wrote a general history from the point of view of a particular life. His two-volume study of Hermann von Boyen, the originator of universal conscription in Prussia, is much more than a biography. But the extensive discussions of politics, of social and administrative change, of campaigns and diplomatic negotiations, are tied to an account of one man's development, successes and failures. It is as though works with such titles as *Robespierre and the State* or *Carnot and the Emergence of Modern France* constituted our major interpretations of the French Revolution.

Reasons for this difference in the treatment of crucial and nearly simultaneous segments of the French and the German past are not hard to find. One cause may be the bourgeois, idealistic character of much of German historical writing, which minimizes the determinative influence of social and economic factors, and instead emphasizes ideas, the individual, and the role of such generalities as the state or nation, which are interpreted as possessing a life of their own. I shall return to these objections, which have been raised repeatedly against Meinecke's work. It makes better sense, however, to seek the reasons for dissimilarities in approach to the French Revolution and to German reform not in historiography but in specific differences between the events themselves. The French Revolution occurred in a unified nation. German reactions to the Revolution were fragmented among dozens of political entities; indeed, achieving greater security through a measure of collaboration of autonomous and semi-autonomous German states quickly became one of the challenges of the time. The political fate of the German states in the Revolutionary and Napoleonic era varied from conquest and dissolution to growth under French patronage, and the character of modernization in those states that survived varied as greatly. To overcome the problems posed by this diversity Meinecke rests his interpretation on two collective elements—the force of German cultural development, which, he argues, combined with the power and energy of the Prussian monarchy to create a new political situation in Germany, the precondition for subsequent unification—but he does not fully succeed. His analyses of German culture necessarily encompass all of Germany; his treatment of German social and political change concentrates on one state: Prussia. To this day the political fragmentation of Germany before 1871 presents analytic difficulties to the historian. Even if he concentrates on social and economic rather than on political topics he may find his interpretation warped by the centrifugal force of interactions between a divided people and its many governments.

The absence of revolutionary change in Germany between 1789 and Napoleon's decline adds to the historian's difficulties in treating these years as a distinct period. All forces of continuity notwithstanding, the Revolution marked a deep incision in the history of France. Germany, by contrast, not only lacked political unity, but the adjustments that were undertaken by her many governments were tentative and gradual rather than radical. Unlike the changes that reconstituted French society, they were also partly defensive. They responded not only to the needs for modernization of German society, but at least as much to the needs for warding off French aggression, which for two decades proved to be invincible. The most symbolic and overtly dramatic incidents in German history between

1789 and 1815 were totally unlike the fall of the Bastille, the Tennis Court oath, the execution of Louis XVI, Thermidor, Brumaire, the coronation of Napoleon—they were episodes in the continuing struggle against a foreign power: the cannonade of Valmy, the defeats of Jena and Auerstedt, the occupation of Berlin and Vienna, the victories of Leipzig and Waterloo. In France, too, change was prepared by earlier conditions and even emerged directly from them; but the survival of Germany's old elites, and the moderate nature of her political innovations, favored a view of these years of German history that emphasized continuity and organic development.

Finally, many historians would regard the years of reform and liberation as a failure. That might also be said of the French Revolution, which led to personal despotism, caused the death of hundreds of thousands in two decades of warfare, and transmitted severe social and ideological antagonisms to later generations. Nevertheless, the Revolution fully emancipated the French bourgeoisie, continued the country's administrative centralization, and asserted individual and national ideals that retain their potency to this day, and not only in France. The Revolution was international as well as national in scope, the outcome of centuries of European intellectual and social development. By comparison German achievements seem tame, or at least parochial. In the beginning, certainly, they were more a reaction to the Revolution than an expression of universal concerns—a difference probably not unrelated to the difference between a consolidated France and a fragmented Germany. Helped by their Russian and British allies, the German states destroyed French dominance over Central Europe; but they could not find an adequate political solution for the area. In the international community Germany remained something of a power vacuum, weakened by disunity and the rivalry of her two strongest states; while in internal affairs the signs of political activity that had emerged here and there were blotted out or circumscribed. It was to be one of the decisive factors of modern history that at the turn of the century the German bourgeoisie was still far weaker in size and economically than the French. The promise of greater participation in political life that had been held out to this minority was pushed aside after 1815 by a new bureaucratic absolutism, far less suited to a time of beginning industrialization and rapid population growth than it had been to the conditions of fifty years before. A sense of the disastrous effects that this stunted development was to have on Germany and Europe underlies one of the few books devoted specifically to the period, Walter Simon's *The Failure of the Prussian Reform Movement*. But on the whole, the disappointing, even ominous outcome of this phase of the German past appears to have given historians still another reason for preferring the larger view rather than focus exclusively on the period.

When Meinecke wrote the *Age of German Liberation* in the summer of 1905 this failure was not yet apparent to him. He regarded the years between the 1790's and 1815, which greatly simplified the political map of Central Europe, as a necessary preliminary to national unification—which they proved to be, although in the Napoleonic era a united Germany was neither possible nor generally desired—and he did not doubt that the German empire as it finally evolved was as historically justified and as permanent a political entity as were France, the United Kingdom, or Italy. That is not to say that he was unconcerned about some defects of the new Reich. He welcomed German unification under Prussian leadership, he accepted the institution of the empire as a realistic solution to the age-old problem of the multiplicity of German states; but he opposed the continuing hold of the old elites on much of public life, and advocated the strengthening of representative institutions in Prussia as well as on the national level. He wrote the *Age of German Liberation* both to celebrate the achievements of the early years of the 19th century, and to warn that what he regarded as basic to that achievement—the "alliance" between the Prussian state and the ideas, ideals, and creativity of educated, that is, middle-class Germany—still awaited full implementation. As the introductory chapter of the *Age of German Liberation* indicates, he recognized that the cultural values of the generations of Kant and Goethe, to which he attributed not only spiritual but also political power, were no longer genuinely significant to most modern Germans. But he believed that the middle class retained a stronger sense of them than did any other segment of German society. A revitalized, politically more effective bourgeoisie, a government prepared to adjust to modern conditions, an extension of social justice and humanistically inspired education to the industrial and agricultural proletariat—these seemed to him the still unfulfilled promises of the earlier age. It was only in the framework of a strong state, he believed, that they could be brought to reality.

Readers today may be disturbed by the frank patriotism sounded in some of Meinecke's passages. At the time he wrote, however, few historians whatever their nationality seriously questioned the necessity of the great political systems that had coalesced since the Renaissance. French and English as well as German scholars, though profoundly conscious of their Western heritage, which their own research was probing more deeply every year, could be guilty of cultural and ethnic judgments that are astonishing in their smugness and even brutality. Patriotism of an assertive, increasingly irritated kind was a general European phenomenon, which played a part in the coming of the first World War, but in the *Age of German Liberation* it is at most of marginal importance. The satisfaction that Meinecke felt in the establishment of the second German Reich may be alien to us; but it does nothing to distort his analyses of the development of Prussia before 1789, her reconstitution in the crucible of the Revolution and the Napoleonic era, and the beginning politization of modern German culture.

Another element in the *Age of German Liberation* may be of greater significance. Although the precise differentiation between closely related phenomena was basic to all of Meinecke's work in the history of ideas, in the present book he resorts to such collective generalizations as "spirit," "nation," and "state." In some respects these generalizations are no more than necessary shorthand in a treatment that is both brief and aims to be comprehensive, and the terms are always employed with an awareness of the variety of phenomena underlying them. Nevertheless they can be dangerous analytic devices because they posit what may be called an operational unity of attitude, intent, or action. Of the three, "nation" and "spirit" play a relatively unambiguous role. Meinecke uses "nation" in something akin to its original apolitical or prepolitical sense of people living in the same geographic area, sharing historical traditions and cultural attributes. Occasionally the term is given its narrow 18th-century meaning of cultural and social elite, more often it stands for the German people as a whole; and the growing link between the former and the latter is one of the main themes of the work. "Spirit" usually refers to achievements of German intellectuals and artists that acquire some permanence, that is, a degree of general acceptance, and that despite individual differences evince a basic affinity—an affinity that increases, Meinecke suggests, the more clearly their work expresses the characteristics of the nation.

That these characteristics can be given different form, that they may even be contradictory, Meinecke reveals with admirable clarity in the book's third chapter, "German Cultural Life and the Prussian State before 1806." Indeed, no one has traced the movement of ideas and attitudes from cosmopolitanism to nationalism with deeper insight than he. But in a work as brief as the *Age of German Liberation* some simplification is inevitable. The alternative was to exclude intellectual and cultural factors altogether. That, however, would have resulted in a totally false picture because the leaders of the Prussian reform movement were influenced by the intellectual currents of the age and contributed to them actively as writers, theorists, and even philosophers.

Meinecke's use of the word "state" may present greater difficulties. It was an important advance in historical understanding when toward the end of the Enlightenment men began to regard the European states as political organisms that changed over time in much the same way human beings develop without losing their basic physical and psychological features. This conceptualization, arising from a new sensitivity for the numerous indications of continuity in the past, but also from political theories that had little to do with historical evidence, helped make possible a less abstract, more specific approach to history. Men learned to try to interpret the past more in its own terms than in theirs. But this remarkable declaration of intellectual independence from the pressures of the present was accompanied by an attitudinal danger. The state seen as a historical personality comes to assume a life of its own. From this idea it is only a short step to attributing characteristics and motives to the state that are separate from the characteristics and motives of real people. It is then easily forgotten that at each stage of its existence the state like any other institution is an assemblage of men. Obviously people are influenced by the past and present circumstances of their institution, but it is man who acts, not the state.

Meinecke was far too knowledgeable and intelligent a historian to romanticize the state, and to ignore the impact of individual and class interests on its policies. He never regarded the personification of the state as implying the abdication of personal responsibility. But his analysis of Germany at the beginning of the 19th century assigns great significance to "those supra-individual forces that informed custom and tradition, that lived in the spirit of the people and nation as a whole." He rejected the thesis of the origin of European states developed by the doctrine of natural law, which "argued that the state was created by a contract between men, in other words through a decision of the will guided by reason." Instead he calls our attention to the "strange mixture of light and dark [that] makes up even the individual's ethical and intellectual powers"—with the implication that this mixture is still more strongly present in the state—and emphasizes historical forces "over and beyond the world of conscious action" that direct the paths of men. The conflict between state and individual is stressed throughout the *Age of German Liberation,* but some readers may feel that at times Meinecke assigns too great an authority to the state as a historical personality, a carrier of supra-individual forces.

Before and during the first World War this conception of the state, and especially the Prussian state, was rejected by such Marxist historians as Franz Mehring, although Mehring directed his critique not at Meinecke's work, but at the writings of Meinecke's colleague and friend Otto Hintze.[1] After the war Mehring's criticism was taken up and turned specifically against Meinecke by one of Meinecke's own students, Eckart Kehr. In particular, Mehring and Kehr objected to the absence in studies of the Prussian reform era of a systematic analysis of economic and social factors within the framework of class conflict, which, they asserted, would have shown that the Prussian monarchy, willingly or unwillingly, was subservient to narrow class interests, and that many of the reformers themselves were by no means political idealists.

1. Franz Mehring's review essay of Otto Hintze's history of Prussia, *Die Hohenzollern und ihr Werk,* first appeared in installments in 1915 and 1916. It was reprinted in Mehring's *Gesammelte Schriften und Aufsätze,* iii, Berlin, 1930, pp. 55–135.

Kehr went further and interpreted Meinecke's emphasis on the power of ideas in history as an expression of the continuing political impotence of the German bourgeoisie. At the beginning of this century, he wrote in 1933, the German middle class had the choice of accepting the politics of imperialism or of joining the Social Democrats in opposition. Those unwilling to do either sought escape in a resigned, estheticizing view of the world. This attitude Kehr regarded as the root of Meinecke's method of studying the history of ideas and of its popularity, which made Meinecke the most influential German historian of his generation. By interpreting political and social developments through the vehicle of intellectual history, Meinecke, according to Kehr, had shown

the intellectually disoriented bourgeoisie a way out of its difficulties. In the long run, it is a dead end. But temporarily those who enter it are strengthened and exalted. They feel as if they are on a high mountain from which they look down into a squalid valley where the mob, struggling for its daily bread, is penned in by a narrow horizon and cannot see the light beyond. The superiority complex of the mountain climber is highly developed in the intellectual historian . . . But is this feeling of superiority well-founded? The genesis of the German history of ideas amply demonstrates that it has not concerned itself with things that have had great and direct practical implications. It shies away from ideas that have revolutionized or attempted to revolutionize the world. Democratic ideas in America or France, Socialist ideas in Germany, Bolshevist ideas in Russia are all taboo, for they could only be treated by someone who has formed his own opinion about the social and political situation and has envisaged revolution and collapse in his own country. The historians of ideas are inclined to view such revolutions as repellent, because they force them to make hard choices for or against. Even if they are republicans and democrats, they are politically conservative. They take no interest in workers or employees. The problems of the latter are confined to the day-to-day struggle and are irrelevant at the lofty levels over which the historian of ideas holds sway.[2]

Only a writer committed to the proposition that in the 20th century historical studies were dishonest or antiquated unless they served the cause of socialism could have failed to mention that two of Meinecke's most important books, *Cosmopolitanism and the*

2. Eckart Kehr, "Modern German Historians," in the collection of his essays, *Economic Interest, Militarism, and Foreign Policy: Essays on German History,* edited by Gordon Craig, Berkeley and Los Angeles: University of California Press, 1977, pp. 181–182.

National State and *Machiavellism,* dealt precisely with ideas that had changed the world; but these were ideas that Kehr hated, particularly at a time when Germany was descending into modern barbarism. Actually Kehr was not so much hostile as indifferent to the history of ideas, which he appears to have thought of as unimportant in itself but overly seductive to scholars who might more usefully have explored the economic and social motives of political decisions. It was Hitler's rise to power with the support or acquiescence of many German intellectuals that led Kehr in the days of the Reichstag fire to reject the history of ideas with a vehemence not otherwise found in his writings. Nevertheless his criticism impressed, and still impresses, some historians, who go beyond Kehr in dismissing ideas as nothing but superstructures of the social and economic substructure, a substructure they regard not only as the ultimately significant subject for the historian, but which they interpret in accord with their political convictions and their sense of present and future political needs.

The weakness of this kind of history—its ultimate degeneration into ideology and party slogans—is revealed by parallels to Kehr's attack on Meinecke in the writings of a scholar who in every respect was Kehr's inferior but who held essentially the same position on the issue that matters here, the prominent National Socialist historian Walter Frank. After Frank in 1936 had forced Meinecke to resign from the editorship of Germany's leading historical journal, the *Historische Zeitschrift,* he continued to denounce his works as expressions of a decayed social order. "Capitalist bourgeois society," he wrote, echoing Kehr, "had developed a capitalist bourgeois science of history." Meinecke's analyses emphasized ideas rather than power because Meinecke did not understand power, which he misinterpreted as a combination of ethical and immoral or amoral qualities. On the contrary, power in the right cause could only be good. "A Hamlet-like pallor hung over this declining [bourgeois] culture," whose place had now been taken, Frank declared, by a society and a science of history invigorated by the creed of Nationalsocialism.[3]

Their rhetorical excesses notwithstanding, these polemics contain

3. Walter Frank, "Die deutschen Geisteswissenschaften im Kriege," *Historische Zeitschrift,* CLXIII, No. 1 (1941), pp. 7–8.

some valid points. Any appraisal of a historian's works can appropriately inquire into their author's social and cultural roots. Meinecke himself acknowledged that growing up in the tradition of Prussian neo-humanism was not only a source of strength but also limited his outlook. Kehr was correct when he noted that ultimately Meinecke's sympathies rested with intellectual elites, and Frank rightly suspected that Meinecke's patriotism would not embrace the destruction of Western culture for the sake of German hegemony. The dream of pure, objective history, scorned for different reasons by Kehr and Frank, is indeed a dream. Like every historian, Meinecke had affinities, in which political convictions played a part, that helped determine his choice of topics for research, his selection of sources, and his interpretations. But the impossibility of complete detachment has never meant that the only alternative for history is complete politization.

It remains the most valid criticism of Meinecke's work that he did not balance his analyses of ideas with equally penetrating explorations of social and economic factors, and, further, that, in Felix Gilbert's words, he did not "pursue the study of intellectual trends to an analysis of the social forces which they represented."[4] His work, like that of every historian, investigates only some, not all, facets of his topic. But that is not to say that Meinecke disregarded the social and economic spheres. The *Age of German Liberation* contains precise analyses of social conditions, and Meinecke's evaluation of the course of urban and agrarian reform, far from perfunctory, is that of a scholar fully engaged in his task. Such recent critical studies as Hajo Holborn's *History of Modern Germany* closely follow the account of the liberation of the peasants and the reorganization of municipal government in the *Age of German Liberation*.[5] The modern monographic literature on specific aspects of Prussian social and economic history does not so much contradict as complement and expand on Meinecke's concise treatment.[6]

4. Felix Gilbert in his Introduction to the American edition of Meinecke's *Cosmopolitanism and the National State,* Princeton, 1970, p. xiv.

5. Compare, for instance, pp. 78–86 of the present work with Hajo Holborn, *A History of Modern Germany,* ii. New York, 1964, pp. 403–410.

6. Even Kehr's interpretations of the period, though stressing social and economic motives, reveal striking agreements with Meinecke. To give just one example, his

If the *Age of German Liberation* is not solely concerned with abstractions it nevertheless is very much the work of an intellectual historian, who applies his view of the nature and role of ideas to an exceptionally eventful period in the political and military history of Europe. The book's treatment of ideas revolves around three poles. It traces the growth of ideas—the ebb and flow of Fichte's patriotism, for instance, or the slow emergence of a military-bureaucratic concept of the Prussian state. Ideas, however, are interpreted not only as steps in the intellectual development of an individual, a group, or nation; they are also seen as phenomena that deserve to be studied for their own sake and in their own terms. Finally, the book examines ideas in their cultural as well as socio-economic context. The *Age of German Liberation* takes ideas seriously—in themselves, as expressions of a continuing process of intellectual development, and as forces for political, social, and economic change.

This many-faceted approach is developed in terms that despite the outdated elements I noted earlier have lost none of their logic and interpretive force. An example is the genetic rather than static method of intellectual history, employed both in the interpretation of individual intellectual systems and of the development of broadly held beliefs. Another is Meinecke's use from the opening paragraph on of the comparative method, which opposes and contrasts individuals, societies, and even historical periods to define specific German conditions more sharply and fit the German experience into the context of world history. Yet another is Meinecke's rejection of closed historical categories in favor of a comprehensive analysis that tries to demonstrate the interdependence and interaction of all aspects of the period—political, military, economic, and cultural.

The integrative character of Meinecke's analysis benefited from the position the *Age of German Liberation* assumes in his oeuvre. He wrote the book after twenty years of archival research in Prussian administrative and political history, and just before launching on his great innovative studies in the history of ideas, for which, in some

---

characterization of Stein in his essay "The Genesis of the Prussian Bureaucracy and The *Rechtsstaat*," Kehr, p. 146, reads like a paraphrase of the analysis of Stein in the *Age of German Liberation*.

respects, it is a preliminary sketch. The *Age of German Liberation* bridges the two major phases of Meinecke's scholarly life, and contains elements of both, just as it links two major forces—state power and cultural and intellectual development—in Germany at the beginning of the 19th century. The little book thus offers both an interpretation of a crucial period of Germany's past and an introduction to the thought and method of one of her great historians.

Chronology

1740	Frederick II, King of Prussia. Prussia conquers Silesia.
1774	Goethe: *The Sorrows of Werther.*
1780	Stein enters Prussian service.
1786	Gneisenau enters Prussian service. Frederick II dies, and is succeeded by Frederick William II.
1789	Fall of the Bastille.
1791	Hardenberg enters Prussian service.
1792	France declares war on Austria and Prussia. Humboldt: *Ideas on an Attempt to Determine the Limits of the State's Authority.*
1794	France conquers Belgium and the left bank of the Rhine.
1795	Final partition of Poland. Prussia and France sign the Peace of Basel; Austria continues the war against France until 1797. Kant: *On Perpetual Peace.*
1797	Frederick William II dies, and is succeeded by Frederick William III.
1799	Schleiermacher: *Lectures on Religion.*
1801	Scharnhorst enters Prussian service.
1805	Napoleon invades southern Germany and Austria. Occupation of Vienna. Battle of Austerlitz.
1806	Prussia annexes Hanover. England declares war on Prussia. Napoleon organizes the Confederation of the Rhine. Dissolution of the Holy Roman Empire of the German Nation.

Prussian ultimatum to Napoleon. Battles of Jena and Auerstedt. The French occupy Berlin and all of Prussia except East Prussia and parts of Silesia and Pomerania.

1807 Peace of Tilsit between France and Prussia. Former Prussian and other German territories are combined into the new kingdom of Westphalia and the Grand Duchy of Warsaw.

Stein is appointed first minister in Prussia.

Scharnhorst is appointed head of the Military Reorganization Commission.

Emancipation of the peasants in Prussia.

Fichte: *Addresses to the German Nation.*

1808 Paris Convention limits the size of the Prussian army and fixes the war indemnity to be paid to France.

Reform of the central administrative agencies in Prussia. Stein's municipal ordinance. Tax reforms linked with the promise of a constitution.

Stein is dismissed, and is succeeded by Altenstein and Dohna.

Kleist: *Die Hermannsschlacht.*

1809 Humboldt is appointed head of education and religious affairs in Prussia.

Austria declares war on France. Insurrections in Germany. Napoleon occupies Vienna. Peace of Schönbrunn.

1810 Hardenberg is appointed chancellor.

The University of Berlin is founded.

France annexes Germany's North Sea coast.

1811 Hardenberg opens the National Assembly of Notables.

The University of Breslau is founded.

1812 Franco-Prussian alliance, which commits Prussia to support the war against Russia.

Invasion of Russia.

Yorck concludes the Convention of Tauroggen, which removes his troops from French command.

1813 Universal conscription in Prussia.

Russo-Prussian alliance against France. War with France.

Scharnhorst dies of wounds received at Grossgörschen.

Battle of Leipzig leads to the French withdrawal from Germany.

1814 Allied Invasion of France. Napoleon abdicates. Occupation of Paris.

Conscription is made permanent in Prussia.

Congress of Vienna.

1815   The Rhineland and part of Saxony are ceded to Prussia.

Frederick William III repeats his promise of a Prussian constitution.

The German Confederation is established.

Napoleon returns from Elba. Battle of Waterloo.

1819   Failure of the constitutional movement in Prussia. Humboldt, Boyen, Beyme, and Grolman are dismissed or leave service.

CHAPTER 1

Introduction

After the collapse of the Holy Roman Empire in 1805 and Prussia's disastrous defeat by Napoleon the following year, Germany's condition was not unlike that of Italy three centuries before. Now as then, a gifted people that only recently had contributed lasting values to mankind was robbed of its political independence and fell prey to foreign despots. Now as then, the intellectual creativity that had recently reached full flowering persisted for a time, as though independent of war and politics. The great masters continued to create according to their inner dictates, while around them their compatriots were crushed. But the immediate successors to Leonardo, Raphael, and Michelangelo already fell far short of the heights their predecessors had reached. Their academic mastery remained impressive, but Leonardo's profound human insight was extinguished. Tradition might salvage the technical achievements of the Renaissance for posterity, but not its soul. That also was true in politics. A favorable constellation enabled the Medicis, who had recently helped catalyze Machiavelli's political conceptions, to establish formal hereditary rule over Florence; but when we look at the statues and portraits of the first Medici grand dukes we see Spanish grandees rather than the unforgettable features of Cosimo the Elder and Lorenzo the Magnificent.

Germany, too, did not remain on the heights she had attained with Kant and Goethe. The force of primal genius, which merged its inwardness with nature and human existence, which triumphed over the paralyzing schism between the self and the world and dissolved it in universal harmony, casting new light and warmth over individual and public life—that force ebbed and abated. The self and the world, culture and nature, again diverged, and today their conflicts oppress us. The varied manifestations of life run their separate ways, divided into countless tiny rivulets. If we look beyond this flux to the spiritual universe inhabited by Goethe or by the Florentines of the 15th century we feel sorrow and frustration.

But at least we want to regain those heights. We do not know whether it is possible, whether we incomplete beings can again become whole; but our need for wholeness cannot be denied, and we are not without strength to strive for it. Nor, flawed though we are, do our efforts to develop the material world lack a certain grandeur. The social and political transformations of our time have created new psychic and moral challenges that fully engage us.

There must be many reasons why in one country the springs of inner life dried up, while in the other, though endangered and diverted, they flowed vigorously on. To interpret these in detail would require exploring centuries of cultural development. But one thing is clear: the survival and continuity of German intellectual life is somehow related to the events between 1807 and 1815—the liberation of Germany from foreign rule, and the transformation of Prussia, her most powerful state, into a freer, more national political entity.

Cultural creativity of the first magnitude does not depend on the existence of powerful national states. But if a society is to maintain creative energy through generations it needs a robust body politic. Political strength serves not only as a shield against foreign aggression; a time comes in the development of modern peoples when the state must be more than a repository of power, when it must sink its foundations deeper into the attitudes and ideals of society, when it must both honor spiritual and moral forces and harness them in its own service as new levers of power. Local and national representative bodies, and national rather than mercenary armies are the most important institutions that now become necessary, but their external forms matter no more than the spirit in which they are conceived and implemented. Much depends on whether society must press its claims on a reluctant government, whether foreign institutions are copied, or whether the loftiest forces of the state and people, in competition and separately, take part in their creation. The stability and health of the whole depends on the extent to which moral and intellectual values are incorporated in the new foundations, on the vigor and spontaneity they generate. The less coercion plays a part in bringing political authority and cultural values together, the greater the benefits to both.

Germany acquired promises of a healthy future during the Wars of Liberation, above all through the achievements and inspiration of the Prussian reform period. In those years culture and intellect freely joined the state, and springs were tapped that irrigated all of German life, far beyond the immediate goal of liberating the country. Earlier achievements, when the German spirit yearned only to perfect itself, undoubtedly reach farther into eternity. But by descending to the state, the spirit not only preserved its own endangered existence as well as that of the state, it secured a reservoir of moral and psychological wealth, a wellspring of creative power for later generations. Our study of the Age of Liberation will attempt to present not only its tangible, immediate results, but also these intangible and inexhaustible qualities.

CHAPTER 2

Frederician Prussia

To understand the alliance between state and spirit in the era of Prussian Reform, we must first recognize the character of the Prussian state as it had developed up to then.

It is surprising that just this state was destined to become the bearer of such an alliance, because on the whole Prussia was an autocratic, military kingdom, shaped by and for war and conquest. Prussia was not even a power based on a contiguous area and an essentially homogeneous population, but an aggregate of various, in part widely scattered lands and peoples, with considerable cultural and religious differences, further separated by significant social and economic barriers. The unifying and vital principle of the whole rested in the dynasty's gift of leadership, in the qualities that the Great Elector, Frederick William I, and Frederick the Great had brought to the state. They accumulated their territories by adroit, daring, often unscrupulous and brutal policies, and by themselves leading their armies, which gave them heroic stature. From these territories their carefully organized bureaucracy wrested the means for maintaining an army that in proportion to the population was far in excess of forces raised by other states. A brisk, penetrating air pervaded this state of soldiers and officials, which had developed into a major power without the physical basis for such growth, and which more tightly and relentlessly than others had to harness its energies to maintain this position. Nevertheless, its monarchs could not simply exploit their people, but had to govern according to the motto of an ancient Sassanide ruler: "No kingdom without soldiers, no soldiers without money, no money without a people, no people without justice." The state also had to rely on the population's moral qualities. It required a sense of honor in its officers, stimulated reliability and a concept of duty in its officials, trained its subjects to be industrious, and sought to develop their minds through education. But what did all this signify compared with the ideals of German poetry and philosophy? Here, a shrewdly calculating practical sense, sobriety, and matter-of-fact virtue: there, an unforced, joyous lifting of the spirit, an unconstrained flowering of all inner forces. Here, brittle, austere nature, artfully controlled by commands and rules, while there all existing rules and constraints were broken so that the fullness of primal nature could be embraced. It was not only Frederick the Great's French tastes that caused him to reject the new German poetry. The spirit of his state contained an element that was alien, almost hostile to German culture. The great poets tolerated the great king more than he tolerated them, because consciousness of their own riches made them generous. Goethe could appreciate the impressive qualities of Frederick's personality and governmental apparatus without repugnance. "It is an agreeable feeling," he wrote in 1778 to his friend Frau von Stein from Frederick's Berlin, "to sit by the springs of war at the moment when they threaten to overflow." He took pleasure in what he saw, and showed his inner superiority by the tenor of his appreciation: "If I can only give a clear account of the great music box, turning and ringing before us. From the movement of the puppets one can infer the hidden wheels, especially the old master-cylinder, inscribed *Fr[idericus] R[ex]* with a thousand pegs and pins, which emits these melodies one after the other."

The impression of artificiality produced by the Prussian monarchy is strengthened when we examine the details of its political and social structure. Its military and bureaucratic institutions were superimposed on institutions of an earlier political epoch, which had been motivated by a basically different spirit. Two disparate elements were joined together; the older was subordinated to the more recent, had been adapted to it and was utilized by it, but nevertheless was only partly divested of its original character. Now it served purposes for which it had never been created.

This older element was the small territorial state as it had developed in Germany to the mid-seventeenth century. This political type had been dualistic, in the sense that the power of the prince and of the Estates opposed each other, creating two separate political spheres. The Estates were politically privileged classes of the population, in Brandenburg primarily the landed nobility and also the city magistrates. As elsewhere, they had their own financial administration, their own treasuries separate from the sovereign's, and what monies they granted him were considered voluntary and extraordinary contributions. Practice often diluted the principle, and an awareness of shared responsibilities might cause ruler and Estates to collaborate, but neither could feel absolute solidarity with the interests of the country as a whole. Each disputed the other's right to represent the country. This irreconcilable dispute forced each side into selfish consolidation of its special interests. The sovereign thought of his dynasty, of the glory and wealth of his house, of advancing new hereditary territorial claims, while the Estates above all guarded their social and economic authority over the lower levels of the population. The sovereign himself was a major landowner. The revenues from his domains were the only relatively productive source over which he freely disposed. According to the prevailing view, these revenues and the incomes from certain sovereign privileges, coinage, customs duties, and the like, were to suffice for his needs. It is characteristic that the central organs of his state administration originated in court offices; many of his representatives in the provinces were local nobles, who often felt themselves to be members of their Estate as much as servants of their prince. Obviously such a dualistic state structure could not generate much energy in domestic or foreign affairs; of necessity it was oriented toward a quiet, conservative existence and peaceful policies. Men talked of the storm winds in the outside world, and bowed low to avoid being swept away by them. The spiritual side of life was cultivated above all through massive piety in the form of orthodox Lutheranism.

The dynastic interests of the Hohenzollern became the means of broadening this narrow existence. The acquisition of Cleves and Mark in the west, and of East Prussia in Germany's extreme east, raised the Hohenzollern into a new political and intellectual sphere. They were drawn into every issue of German and European politics. If they wished to preserve the exposed territories they had inherited, they had to reinforce the original basis of their power and considerably extend it. Since they now ruled regions of differing faiths, they had to free themselves from the confessional narrowness of 16th-century territorial princes. In 1613, the Elector Johann Siegmund joined the Reformed Church, which meant that he had at least one foot in the camp of politically aggressive, advancing Protestantism. But it was to prove equally significant that the power of the Lutheran Estates in Brandenburg compelled him to relinquish the right of forcing his subjects to adopt his new faith. He did not yet exercise true tolerance, but his religious policies were modern, and potentially rewarding. On the whole, this course was also followed by his successors. When Pietism, the first wave of the new inner life in Protestant Germany, emerged toward the end of the 17th century, it found a special welcome in pacific Brandenburg-Prussia, in which different confessions were tolerated. Pietism was succeeded by rationalism, which had even greater affinity with the now absolutist, military spirit of the Prussian state, and merged with it in various ways. And yet rationalism was to be the historical steppingstone leading to the most magnificent achievement of the German mind since the Reformation. We have already suggested, and will have to demonstrate further on, that this step was difficult and meant a struggle between the old and the new. Here we need only indicate that Brandenburg-Prussia's ecclesiastical politics, as they had been historically conditioned, included the possibility of adapting to Germany's growing intellectual life. The austere military state of the 18th century could more readily transform itself into the culturally rich state of the era of reform and of the 19th century because political conditions had earlier forced it to adopt toleration.

Hence the earliest events that shook the old territorial state from its sleep contained the seeds of blossoms that were to flower two centuries later. In the meantime other forces asserted their dominance in Brandenburg. As the Great Elector went about establishing a standing army and putting himself "in good position," he had to intimidate the Estates in his various territories into granting him the right of regular taxation. His success gave rise to everything that followed. From the firm base provided by the power to tax grew the administrative agencies required by the new army as well as the new army taxes themselves, until the new institutions overarched the old territorial state. The Great Elector's commissaries were not satisfied with accepting revenues from the Estates, but themselves began to levy and administer taxes, and above all invaded the weaker of the Estates, the towns and their administrative organs, on which much of the towns' financial capabilities depended. They reformed and regulated, abolished old abuses of the oligarchic town governments, but also suppressed the spirit of municipal independence. The landed nobility fared better. While the nobles could no longer effectively oppose the sovereign in the provincial diets, as possessors of patrimonial justice and police they retained authority in their manors; they were lords over their hereditary serfs, the peasants tied to the soil, from whose compulsory labor they benefited now as before. But they could no longer enlarge their estates, as they would have liked, by incorporating peasant land, because the kings now required not only money for their growing army but also people. Frederick William I assigned a recruiting district to each regiment, from which it drew some of its replacements. This was the second new obligation exacted from the land, a duty completely alien to the old territorial state: some of its young men were forced to become soldiers. The older military arrangements had been dualistic. The hired troops constituted the actual instrument of the prince's policies and wars; beside them existed the feudal obligation of vassals and subjects to serve, spelled out in manifold clauses and militarily of little use, more the country's defense organization than the sovereign's, wholly characteristic of the peaceful posture of the older territorial state. This dualism was now overcome, the militia units disappeared, and the old Germanic sense of the general obligation to fight that had faintly survived in them was used to help create the single royal army that would fight the battles of Frederick the Great.

In other areas of the state, too, the former dualism was gradually eliminated. The sovereign's new agents, created to administer the new army taxes, at first existed independently beside the older financial and administrative authorities for the domain holdings, formerly the main sources of the prince's income. In these domain agencies the traditions of the older territorial and Estate era continued, while the modern commissariats represented the more energetic and disciplined tendencies of the military state. To remove the duality, which paralyzed administration in many ways, Frederick William I combined both services in 1723. From now on, the General Superior Finance, War, and Domain Directory—the so-called General Directory—functioned as the country's supreme administrative and financial authority, and the War and Domain

Boards as the subordinate provincial agencies. The organs of the old and of the new concept of the state were thus united under the primacy of the latter. Soon the intense administrative energy with which the commissaries had launched their work invaded the leisurely, patriarchal methods of the domain agencies. The administrative wheels turned faster to create money for the army. But the royal will alone drove on and steered the whole, not only with general directives but also by intervening in seemingly insignificant details; if some wheel or cog jammed the sovereign himself might straighten things out. These interventions in the minutiae of the 18th-century Prussian administration have often been criticized; but for the system they were necessary. Only in this way could resistant matter be pressed into the forms that the military state of Frederick William I and his son required. For as we have noted, the state was and remained an edifice raised on foundations of a very different structure. A closer look reveals this in every area: everywhere the old projects into the new, everywhere we encounter institutions that disrupt the unity of the whole and work against the concentration of energies resting in the people and the state. The older institutions were reshaped and adapted to the state's new purpose, or they were weakened and repressed, but their original nature still persisted beneath the surface.

To begin with, Frederick William I's great administrative reform was far from total. The General Directory, and its subordinate agencies did not exert control over the entire internal administration of the country. Together with the War and Domain Boards the "governments," the old supreme provincial authorities, continued to exist. Although severely circumscribed in their administrative authority, and limited primarily to their jurisdiction as the highest provincial courts, they were endowed with remnants of their old territorial glory. More important, the organization of the General Directory itself reflected a former age when the various territories of the prince were united only in his person. For the most part, administration was still organized not according to function but on provincial lines. For each three or four adjoining provinces a provincial department, headed by a minister, was created within the General Directory. The system recognized the uniqueness of the judicial, social and economic conditions of each region, based on its historical development, a reality that was accepted and that was dealt with by individual ministers of the General Directory becoming specialists for their particular region. This system did not indicate a fundamental reformist zeal that wished to build a unified state. That goal did not yet exist; nor, probably, did the capability to achieve it. To wrest the means for supporting the military state and the dynasty's power politics from these disparate territories was already an enormous achievement.

To be sure, in the course of the 18th century provincial departments were joined by other agencies. Frederick the Great added several functional departments to administer certain activities for the monarchy as a whole, above all that of commerce and trade, and that of mining. These modern economic concerns pointed beyond narrow provincial boundaries to a stage when the entire territory of the state would be a truly unified economic entity. But Frederick stopped halfway; by permitting functional and provincial departments to coexist he turned the basically simple structure of the General Directory into something complex and impenetrable, while Silesia, the crown's new valuable acquisition, was not administered by the General Directory at all. Hence, even more than in his father's time, the unity of the whole rested not in the state's administrative institutions, but in the sovereign personally. In his office the reports and budgets of the various administrative bodies converged. Only he completely surveyed the whole, and channeled the accumulated resources toward his other great area of concern—the army. Here the massive power of the Prussian state, gathered in his hands, could indeed appear to his time and to posterity as truly unified. But even in his lifetime a farsighted contemporary noted that in reality the Prussian monarchy was only an aggregate of larger and smaller states. After Frederick's death, as weaker hands sought to govern in his manner, it became increasingly apparent that this state lacked political unity.

Was at least the tool of his power politics, the army, for whose maintenance everything was designed, a uniform creation cast in one mold? On the battlefield, it was. In accord with the tactics and operational methods of the time the all-powerful will of the supreme commander determined when the mass of soldiers, ranged in long, thin, closely packed ranks, advanced, fired, and attacked. The separate components of the army were allowed little independence in battle. More comprehensively than in modern warfare, the controlling reins converged in the hands of the commander. For

Frederick's ultimate purpose, in short, the army formed as compact an entity as the state as a whole formed a single political force in European affairs. To the outside world it presented a threatening front, but its internal structure was as heterogeneous as was the basis of the state. Two entirely different elements composed the rank and file: the draftee, usually drawn from the peasantry, and the hired foreigner. The native son, brought up in patriarchal sentiments of awe and obedience, who was simply transferred from the authority of his squire to the drill of his supreme commander, was a man very different from the unreliable foreign mercenary, usually an individual with a checkered past, who could only be controlled by a frequently brutal system of discipline. Frederick knew perfectly well that his natives were more reliable, but he would not draw the consequence and recruit the entire army from his peasants. He welcomed foreigners because the marriages into which they were permitted to enter helped populate the country. He did not wish to overtax Prussia's draft districts, these "apples of his eye"; nor was he willing to withdraw too many workers from trade and agriculture, whose output filled his treasury. He could maintain his international position only by severely economizing his resources, and thus he was not above accepting and utilizing the refuse of other nations. Actually it was far from easy to obtain this poor human material in the desired numbers, because Prussian recruiting officers were not welcome abroad, and neighboring princes did not want to lose their subjects. That Frederick stubbornly continued foreign recruitment even after the experience of the Seven Years War shows that he thought it indispensable. But it also shackled his army and its operations, and greatly inhibited the free unfolding of military energies. To maintain discipline and to prevent his soldiers from deserting, he could not allow them to requisition and forage in enemy territory. If at all possible, therefore, they had to be provisioned from depots, which made necessary immense baggage trains that paralyzed the movements of the armies. Nor could his soldiers be allowed the same freedom of movement on the battlefield that skirmishing and open order affords the modern soldier. Because they were so unreliable, they had to move and fight in the greatest possible cohesion, had to be drilled until they were machines. With such armies, compelled to use such tactics, one could not risk costly battles too often, because casualties were difficult to replace. Consequently, strategy became highly artificial. Battle could not be avoided entirely, of course, but one tried to achieve as much as possible by demonstration and maneuver. A concept of strategy developed which held that it was not essential to crush the enemy. Rather his forces should be kept in check, one should protect or threaten as much territory as possible in order to divide the enemy's troops—though admittedly only by fragmenting one's own. In this way the fire and energy of war were dampened, its means and forces diluted. The ultimate reason was that the sources of military energy, the army's replacements, flowed so meagerly and required so much protection. The power base was too small.

The indispensable foreign mercenary was a remnant of the time of the Landsknechte and the hired armies of the Thirty Years War. Though now organized and tamed, this restless element did not stop chafing at the bit, and imperceptibly it checked the unfolding of the state's military energy and therefore political power. Here we see the discrepancy in the structure of the new military state with particular clarity, that contradiction between its new purposes and old foundations, which had been only artificially and incompletely adapted. As long as similar though less extreme conditions prevailed in other states, the contradiction was not apparent. But when this ceased to be the case, the system in Prussia lost its historical and political justification.

Actually the system could be implemented only because another historical element of older origin had been adapted and made useful to the purposes of the military state: the Brandenburg-Prussian nobility. The nobility's power as an Estate, its claims to share political authority, had been crushed; for this it was compensated not only by continuation of its social and economic privileges, but with the honors and advantages attached to service in the army. The noble's personal interest in the new military state was engaged, and his attitude to state and army changed. Young nobles brought the army a wealth of elemental energy, in effect they became its moral backbone. The Prussian monarchy disciplined and educated many segments of the older territorial state, but the taming of the nobility was by far the most successful and consequential achievement. Of all elements in Prussian society, the nobility became the first to enter into a true relationship with the new concept of the state, a relationship based on conviction, not mere passive obedience, and one that forcefully expressed genuine beliefs. From a merely social and politically self-serving elite, the nobility became something akin to a national class. To use Frederick's own words, it was being infused not only with *esprit de corps* but with an *esprit de nation*. Its narrow provincial pride melted on the battlegrounds of Frederick's wars. The bond between nobility and the crown grew to be so strong that it survived all changes. In the 19th century alliances between the crown and other classes took place, but the historic priority of the bond with the nobility endowed it with a lasting political prerogative.

And yet at what cost was this first national Estate created? Once again it became apparent that the kingdom's base of power was still too narrow to permit thorough reforms of its fundamental institutions. The state had to be satisfied with adapting, crudely and incompletely, older institutions that were no longer suited to its new intentions. It was important to pay the officers, drawn from the landed nobility, not only regularly but also adequately, and thus to satisfy their material needs. Considering the economy and taxation system of the time, it was a major achievement of Frederick William I to pay his soldiers regularly, but the pay itself could only be meager. An older, primitive practice was adopted to provide officers from company commanders up with a comfortable income, and thus at least to hold out the possibility of security to all officers. This was the system of "company economy." Originally colonels and company commanders had been business entrepeneurs who concluded a contract with the prince for raising and maintaining their unit. The ruler provided the funds, checked whether the officers carried out what they had promised, and left them any surplus. Gradually the economic independence of the company commanders was reduced, yet they retained some funds that were managed in the old way and continued to pocket any savings. A captain with a pay of 800 talers, could easily increase his peacetime income to 1500 or 2000 talers, and since every fieldgrade officer in the regiment retained the "ownership" of a company, he had a sinecure. But these sinecures returned a profit only in peacetime; during war everything went for the needs of his troops. So curiously had this institution changed that a source of profit for the military entrepreneurs of the Thirty Years War now constituted a heavy financial drain on the state for the benefit of the more tightly controlled captains of the 18th and beginning 19th centuries. Once again the adaptation of a traditional institution to the ends of the military state in the final analysis worked against those very ends, because it weakened the will to fight of the more senior officers.

Let us return from military affairs to social and economic life. The state, I have said, protected the nobility's position as patrimonial lords over the peasants, but also protected the peasants by preventing their small holdings from being incorporated into the noble estate. The state desired a robust, productive peasantry, above all because it provided recruits to the army, and because peasants paid the "contribution," the army tax, exacted from rural areas, from which the landed nobility was largely exempt. Again traditional social and economic conditions were retained and at the same time tailored to the needs of the army and the monarchy. But could the old means fully achieve the new goals? Shackled as they were, the peasants could not readily become economically independent. The manual and team labor they owed the lord was performed grudgingly and poorly. Their labor was compulsory but at the same time uneconomic. Landowners knew this, and some were beginning to replace the compulsory labor of their peasants with work done for hire by the rural proletariat.

Another device to protect the status of the nobility and its economic conditions was to prohibit or make it difficult for wealthy bourgeois to buy a nobleman's estate. But again this remedy, derived from traditional social attitudes, was two-edged, because those nobles who wanted or had to sell their land were faced with limited markets and consequently lower prices.

It would be going too far here to examine other privileges left to the nobility, and show that in the final analysis they damaged the nobility itself or at least hurt economic life in general. Yet Frederick William and his son desired to develop all branches of the economy, agriculture, manufacture, and commerce, and to awaken the energy and enterprise of their subjects. They were not simply in favor of the nobility and against the middle class. But because in their urban economic policies they tied themselves too closely to institutions created under former territorial conditions, ends and means came into conflict here too.

In the same centuries of transition from the Middle Ages to modern times when the German territorial state was created, German towns also fought to gain and consolidate an economically privileged position, a process that led to a sharp separation between country and town. Towns dominated the economy of the surrounding countryside, prevented the development of competing commercial activity in rural areas, and monopolized the grain trade. In the same monopolistic spirit they conducted trade with foreign merchants for the benefit of native producers and consumers, and organized business activity within their walls by retaining guild restrictions. Given the primitive economic conditions of the time, this system of coercion and exclusion for the sake of economic autonomy undoubtedly helped develop the power of the German bourgeoisie; but it also deepened the chasm that separated the middle class from other groups in society. Nothing would be less accurate than to regard the German burgher of the 16th to the 18th century as a modern, liberal citizen, as the champion of social and political equality. The basis of the middle class, like that of the nobility, was privilege and exclusiveness.

These were the conditions that confronted the great architects of the Brandenburg-Prussian state, and in the main they retained them because they could be adapted to the immediate ends of the crown. If the nobility supplied the officers, and the peasants the best soldiers, the towns had to provide the larger part of the necessary funds. When the Great Elector succeeded in imposing his army taxes, the Brandenburg towns preferred to raise their share not, as did the countryside, by land- and building taxes, the *contributionale,* but through a series of taxes on consumption and trade, the so-called excise. This tax was more attuned to urban conditions, it burdened the individual less and was easier to increase than the rural contribution. The government therefore soon took over the excise administration from the towns, and now controlled a source of income that depended directly on the prosperity of the urban economy, and thus favored the preservation of the towns' special economic status. No significant commercial activity was allowed to develop in the countryside, because it would have reduced the municipal excise. The only change from earlier times was that once each town had isolated itself and pursued its own protectionist policies, now the government defended all towns and separated them from the rest of the country. The economic policies of the individual town were replaced by the economic policies of the state; the economic system as a whole, however, remained unchanged.

The special privileges that a town had once acquired might be reduced in the interest of the urban economy as a whole, some excesses of the guilds could also be trimmed back; but the core of the old institutions was maintained and now served new ends.

The towns proved useful to the new purpose in other ways. Soldiers could be quartered in the houses of the burghers. The garrisons increased the amount of the excise. Walls and sentries needed to inhibit smuggling and collect the excise also prevented desertion. Retired soldiers and invalids could be given municipal employment. The poorer members of the urban population could be drafted into the army, whereas those groups in trade and commerce whose well-being mattered most to the state received broad exemptions. Exempting craftsmen and the higher levels of the bourgeoisie from military service was a new privilege that fitted well with the traditional spirit, and at the same time compensated for the loss of former rights, particularly for the loss of municipal freedom and independence.

The towns surrendered their freedom to the bureaucracy, to the tax councilors, and to the War and Domain Boards, which now directed and supervised the municipal administration. The old oligarchic, corporate structures of the municipal constitution remained, just as the old constitutions of the Estates were, in general, not abolished. But one like the other became a mere shadow.

The autonomy of the towns had grown in step with their privileged economic status. Historically speaking both belonged together. In the long run, was it possible to break one, while preserving and merely bending the other? The towns had attained economic prosperity under self-government in an atmosphere of freedom. Could bureaucratic guardians call forth a new flowering? The state, after all, set limits beyond which they would not move. Undoubtedly the bureaucracy wanted to achieve much, and it prepared the way for things to come, but the future like the past could truly flourish only in freedom. What was needed was to bring industry and business with strong capitalization into the urban economy, as was happening in Western Europe. The economic lead that the West had attained induced Frederick the Great to attempt the same development. Since the economic initiative did not come from below, he and his officials had to attract entrepeneurs by grants and governmental support. Since the new industries could not be pressed into the guild mold, they were allowed freer forms. Old and new economic styles now existed side by side, leading to friction between the guild masters, who employed a limited number of journeymen, and the entrepeneurs who were allowed as many workers as needed. Some new industries also pushed beyond the town walls, but it was thought too risky to remove this barrier completely because most institutions remained predicated on the separation of country and town. What was achieved despite these handicaps, for example the growth of the silk industry—a special concern of Frederick's—was noteworthy, but remained a fragile development. The intelligence and energy of the bureaucracy simply could not take the place of middle-class drive and enterprise, which was throttled everywhere by an atmosphere that simultaneously exerted old and new pressures.

CHAPTER 3

German Cultural Life
and the Prussian State Before 1806

Thus Prussians lived simultaneously in the old, dualistic territorial state, and the new military monarchy, in the inherited patriarchal attitudes of the one and the newly imposed military-bureaucratic discipline of the other. The picture grows even more varied and discordant when we realize that the educated higher classes lived in yet a third world, a wholly new realm, untouched by the state, where the individual shed his political and social cloak and man himself stood revealed as the origin, measure, and end of all values. While in these circles men might speak of "society" and of the individual's relation to society, they did not so much think of historically developed social institutions and customs as of the social intercourse between individuals, to which they attributed greater significance than we do today. Society was a marketplace where men could freely give and partake of human values. And that conception was not entirely illusory. Within the narrowly restricted, corporative society of the old Estates existed a new world of free individuals, of personalities seeking and finding themselves, a literate, book- and letter-writing society. These men and women reigned above ordinary reality like the gods on Mount Olympus; what happened on earth below reached them only as an echo. It is striking how vaguely the conditions and events of the real world are mirrored in their letters. Occasionally interest is expressed in them, but usually events are transformed into general principles and ideas; the letters are submerged in philosophical and esthetic reflection in which the whole world appears more beautiful, spiritual, and pure. At least men wished for such a world, in which, as Wilhelm von Humboldt said at the time, "everything corporeal [was] mere envelope and tool," in which even the peasant and worker were artists who pursued their calling with inner conviction. And if in real life the class arrogance of the nobility was encountered, one could recall Goethe's words in *Wilhelm Meister*: "Do not chide them for it. They seldom attain a heightened perception of the happiness that we recognize as the highest, the happiness that flows from the inner wealth of nature." By "nature," of course, Goethe did not mean harsh, discordant reality but "divinity, which lets the corporeal dissolve in the spirit."

In the meantime the French Revolution and its wars shook the world. Men certainly allowed themselves to be shaken by this drama, but they reacted to it as to a drama on the stage. After the Peace of Basel of 1795, northern Germany enjoyed neutrality, lying like an island amid the stormy European sea. Later Goethe looked back longingly on these years, which allowed the individual to develop in his own way. The period of neutrality, says Ranke, helped provide scope for the young shoots of literature to grow and mature. If men had already been forced to concentrate on politics and the state, their free, infinitely aspiring intellectual life might have been constrained too soon, and perhaps we would have been deprived of the classical decade from 1795 to 1805. As it was, the major changes in international affairs constituted simply one subject among many for the freely creative, interpretive mind. Political events were discussed, sometimes even with burning zeal, but as the nature philosopher Steffens later characterized these debates, "everything was doctrine, theory, principle, the future; no one as yet had any idea of a political present that called for action."[1] In the external world, in the meantime, one German territory after another was lost. This scarcely disturbed the philosophers. Do you really believe, Fichte asked sarcastically in 1793, that the German artist or peasant much cares whether from now on the artist or peasant from Lorraine or Alsace finds his town and village listed in geographical textbooks in the chapter on the German Empire?[2] In their youth the early Romantics, too, were still strongly influenced by cosmopolitanism.

1. Henrik Steffens (1773–1845), professor at the University of Halle, and a member of the Prussian reform movement.

2. Johann Gottlieb Fichte (1762–1814), the philosopher.

Wackenroder mocked Brandenburgian patriotism, and Novalis explained: Germanness is cosmopolitanism alloyed with the most robust individuality.[3]

Thus the political boundaries of the Empire and of the Prussian state were ignored at the very time that philosophers and poets enjoyed the protection afforded by the Prussian sphere of power. It was never completely forgotten that nationality and German values existed, but here, too, men allowed "the corporeal to dissolve in the spirit," and resisted the idea that the "organization of the state" could also be a "national institution." An important difference, said Wilhelm von Humboldt, remains between the two, in that the latter allows greater freedom in entering into, modifying, and dissolving relations. Like society, the nation was a spontaneous, natural union of like-minded individuals. The community was the means, but the end was the spiritual education of the individual toward energy and beauty.

Intellectual roots reaching far back in time explain how society, the state, and the nation could be seen so preponderately from the viewpoint of individual need, how the firm, organic bonds that connected society, state, and nation, and the individual to them, could be overlooked. It was precisely the organic aspects of the state and society that were denied by the doctrine of natural law, which can be traced back to the Middle Ages and antiquity. This doctrine argued that the state was created by a contract between men, in other words through a decision of the will guided by reason. Accordingly, it was by their personal action, in the clear light of consciousness, that men banded together to create the state. In the 18th century, the Enlightenment carried these ideas further. It saw the history of mankind as the struggle of virtue and vice, of reason and folly, sometimes optimistically, sometimes with a more pessimistic tendency, but usually without understanding the strange mixture of light and dark that makes up even one individual's ethical and intellectual powers—without fully understanding, above all, that beyond the world of conscious action stronger, historical forces direct the paths of men. This rationalistic individualism was

3. Wilhelm Wackenroder (1773-1798), author of a popular romantic tract, *Confessions of an Art-Loving Friar*; Novalis—that is, Friedrich von Hardenberg (1772-1801)—poet and author of a seminal work in the social philosophy of Romanticism, *Christendom and Europe*.

succeeded toward the end of the 18th century by idealistic individualism, the world-view of Goethe, Schiller, and Wilhelm von Humboldt. It enormously deepened conceptions of the essence and actions of the individual, replaced external categories of virtue and vice, reason and the irrational, with vital forces rooted in the unconscious and nature, forces that strove toward clarity of the spirit and in a sense replaced the flat, horizontal structure of the soul with a vertical one, and its parallel or discordant drives with a hierarchic, concordant harmony. This change also cast new light on the historical world, on the life of peoples in general. Here, too, men began to sense an inseparable mixture of spirit and nature, and the significance of those supra-individual forces that informed custom and tradition, the institutions of former generations, that lived in the spirit of the people and nation as a whole. But everything was still in its first beginnings. Although enthusiastically reaching for the new, one fell back often enough into old, overly rational ways of thinking. Above all, a stage had been reached in which the individual was just becoming conscious of his own hidden wealth; he luxuriated in the joys of discovery and believed that a limitless empire lay before him. The growth of individuality, the highest, most symmetrical development of its various powers into a totality, the distinctiveness of each talent and culture—to achieve these, Humboldt thought, was the true purpose of man, on which his greatness ultimately depended, the goal toward which man must eternally strive. Man's striving for individuality, and beyond it only all-powerful, unvanquished fate, which dispensed the highest happiness as well as the greatest misery—that was the grandiose idealized image of life as it appeared from these heights. Understandably, it could not yet accommodate the concrete forces of history. The actual state, actual society, the actual environment— what did these mean to him who recognized only fate as being stronger than himself and his soul? Such intermediary powers were disdained; men felt too free, too lofty to enter readily into the restrictions of actual life. What gratitude, after all, was owed these intermediaries? Man's inner riches had been acquired through his own power, through his own intellectual effort. No favor by the state or court, as in the France of Louis XIV, nor the patronage of rich and luxury-loving classes, as in the Italian cities, had helped culture and intellect to flourish. The patronage of a ruler like Karl August of Weimar was not really felt as a prince's favor, but more as the favor of a friend and human being.[5]

Nevertheless, the German territorial states of the 18th century, and the special conditions they created, indirectly contributed to this attitude. They made it easier for the German spirit to unfold with freedom and autonomy. The German poet or scholar was not showered with rewards and external signs of favor, but he did not require them. He needed a modest, but secure and easily attained subsistence, and there was no lack of small offices and positions. The struggle for existence was not yet very difficult, although existence itself was modest. And no one was too firmly bound to the position he happened to occupy. The bonds were easily knit and easily loosened, to be tied again elsewhere. An ease of movement from land to land prevailed that lent wings to the existence and activities of these men, outwardly and spiritually. Their echo still reverberates in the song from *Wilhelm Meister's Travels*, "From the Mountains to the Hills":

> Where the sun is bright and golden
> Every worry falls aside;
> To allow us room to wander,
> That is why the world is wide.

Fichte bears classical witness to what this meant; in his *Addresses to the German Nation* he recalls: "Everyone was permitted to seek for himself in the whole length and breadth of this land the culture most congenial to him or the sphere of action to which his spirit was best adapted; and talent did not root itself like a tree in the place where it first grew up, but was allowed to seek its own place . . . No German-born prince ever took it upon himself to limit his subjects' fatherland to the mountains and rivers over which he ruled, and to regard his subjects as bound to the soil . . . and so, in spite of many instances of one-sidedness and narrowness in the separate states, Germany as a whole provided the greatest freedom for research and publication that a people ever possessed."

It was also significant that most governments exercised only mild censorship over literature. Of course literature was so unpolitical that the state did not need to worry. And when temporarily, as in Prussia during the time of Wöllner's Religious Edict, suspicion and

4. Karl August, Grand Duke of Saxe-Weimar (1757–1828), Goethe's patron.

persecution of freer intellectual tendencies did arise, neighboring states immediately granted sanctuary to the threatened works.[5]

The freedom of expression, of assembly, of travel created a sense of community among the bearers of the intellectual movement, a sense they themselves already called national feeling, and which in fact became the first level of true national feeling. It was delicate and airy, like a scent, but the scent was of meadows full of exquisite blooms. Now we can really understand Novalis' words that to be German was to be cosmopolitan and simultaneously strongly individualistic. Later, in 1813, Fichte said that until recently only scholars had actually represented the future Germans: through their writings, and through their travels: "Thus the special, noteworthy trait of the German national character lies precisely in the existence of Germans without a state and beyond the state, in their purely intellectual development."

The state, in other words, usually cared little when scholars presented liberal arguments that were at variance with traditional views and with traditional religion. I have already said that Prussia, in particular, was distinguished by religious tolerance, whose origins were closely linked to its political interests. Now I should add that the Prussian state could remain tolerant in part because it continued to grow stronger. The small states of the older territorial period could not forgo religious uniformity among their subjects, because religious divisions only too readily led to political divisions, which reinforced the resistance of the Estates against their princes. The Brandenburg-Prussian military state, on the other hand, had destroyed the power of the Estates, and, conscious of its strength, could be tolerant. Thus the growth of standing armies in Germany may have contributed to the success of the concept of tolerance as much as did the Enlightenment when it penetrated the church and the circle of rulers itself. Frederick the Great's religious indifference would scarcely have prevented him from pursuing intolerant policies if he had regarded them politically expedient. But his army was an instrument of government that made it superfluous for him to impose religious uniformity on his subjects as well.

Thus the division of duties that Frederick maintained in his state, which assigned every group its special function, seemed marvelously

5. Johann Christoph von Wöllner (1732-1800), Prussian minister whose edict of 1788 attempted to reestablish orthodoxy in the Protestant churches.

suited to scholars and writers, to the purveyors of culture. They were not incorporated in the system, but left free since they were not needed and caused no harm. Many of them praised their condition and saw it as the epitome of civilization. How excellent, it was said, that the state raised standing armies and drew on the lower classes for its soldiers. Now the prince can wage his wars, while the burgher follows his trade undisturbed, and the scholar pursues his thoughts.

But gradually this changed. Men could not entirely evade the unrest that the French Revolution had brought into the world. The drama of a nation that was beginning to restructure itself radically, according to philosophical precepts, that proclaimed the state's task and supreme purpose to be the protection of man's inalienable rights—all this was too stirring not to cause intelligent Germans to reflect on their own conditions. But inner impulses as well could create doubts about the social and intellectual divisions of duty under which men lived. Was the free life of the mind, which the scholar enjoyed, to remain a class privilege, like trade and industry for the burgher, and patrimonial authority for the nobility? The new humanistic ideal that had been elevated to the guiding principle in life logically called for general application. One could not forever avoid the fact that the institutions the state imposed on the mass of the population were chains not only for those who struggled to free themselves, but also for those who did not even feel them. Was it not evident that a free peasant and day laborer produced much more than a serf burdened by enforced labor? And—a weightier issue for thoughtful Germans of the time—did not enforced labor also lower the peasant morally? It is the sense of servitude, Fichte called out in 1793, that corrupts the peasant. If Wilhelm von Humboldt hoped that peasant and worker could be free, creative artists, he had first to desire their external freedom, so that they could achieve inner freedom as well. In the 1790's Königsberg above all became a center for such ideas; Kant made no bones of his sympathy for the French Revolution, and Kraus, the national economist, taught the gospel of Adam Smith and free trade to the coming generation of bureaucrats.[6] Perhaps even more significant than the adoptions from

6. Christian Jakob Kraus (1753-1807), professor of political economy at the University of Königsberg.

French and English writers was the changing impact of Kant's philosophy itself. In the late 1780's the critique of pure reason had conquered all minds, but in the following decade Kant's thoughts on practical reason became the catalyst for a genuine social movement. The young officials and officers returned from Kant's lecture hall to their professional duties, resolved to honor the human dignity of even the lowest of their subordinates, to nurture and educate the seed of moral self-determination, which, according to their teacher, lay in every human being. Some thought this could be achieved within existing conditions.

Other, more perceptive, men disagreed, and began to protest against the state. At last political matters aroused genuine passion— not yet the passion that called for action, but an internal revolt of the thinker, who wanted to free himself from the intellectual pressure of what began to be felt as irrational injustice to the individual. Out of this inner need, Wilhelm von Humboldt in 1792 wrote his *Ideas on an Attempt to Determine the Limits of the State's Authority,* and Fichte, in 1793, his *Contributions to Rectify Public Views on the French Revolution.*

They were men of very different temperament. Humboldt wove his precise, firm web of ideas with such calm dialectic, and often in such pale language, that the passion and pride that motivated him are easily overlooked. Fichte, even in these early years, is terse and manly in every line. Humboldt often seems only to think, Fichte often only to demand. In Humboldt we may fail to recognize the energetic will behind the theory. With Fichte we may sometimes forget that his absolute demands were based on intensive, highly structured intellectual efforts. But if we consider both in their entirety, we can understand why, without being aware of each other, they were in surprising agreement on the main issue. Both protested against the existing state, which treated men only as means, not ends. Both forgot the freedom of movement that the state granted scholars, and felt only the pressure that its institutions exerted on men who lived in servitude and were becoming conscious of their servitude. Both empathized with their less fortunate compatriots. "I know," mourned Fichte, "that the state has always worked in every way to accustom us to be machines, not independent beings." "The exaggerated solicitude of the state," Humboldt deduced, "weakens energy and activity in general, and the moral character

[25

[turns] into national uniformity. . . . *Goods* [are produced] at the expense of *vitality.*" We know how true this was of the Frederician state, how systematically Prussia categorized and exploited existing human resources and their institutions for purposes alien to them, and how the state intentionally or unintentionally suppressed the spontaneous energy of its subjects through the violently compressed energy of government.

Hence Fichte and Humboldt fought the state as it was; they did not like Goethe simply ignore or tolerate it. A new epoch was beginning, a new relationship between the state, nation, and the individual; but a clearer understanding of the needs of political organisms was also only in its beginning stages. Fichte and Humboldt did not yet want to reform the state, but to reduce it. Their motto was: As little government and as much individuality as possible. The only task, Humboldt said, that the state should make an object of its activity was the one that citizens cannot carry out on their own: promoting the general security. Government is merely a subordinate means, to which the true end, man, must not be sacrificed. Fichte, too, unequivocally subordinated the state's ultimate purpose to the ultimate purpose of individual existence. That purpose was culture, that is, education through independent activity; neither society nor the state could create culture. "No one becomes cultivated, everyone must cultivate himself." Society, furthermore, provided more and better means for cultural development than did the state.

But was this and could this be their last word? In a sense, yes. Neither Fichte nor Humboldt could move beyond their idea that man's inner freedom is the highest good—nor can mankind today. No one penetrated farther than they into the sphere of the individual and his ultimate tasks; but they did not yet fully grasp the totality of man's qualities and needs. They recognized and valued the spiritual substance of man more than his corporeal qualities, from which and in which he also lives. They perceived the grandiose unity of spirit and nature, but they appreciated the spiritual pole of this unity more than its natural pole. How violently and urgently did Fichte compress his whole conception of the world into the all-creating self! For him the material world seems to exist only to nourish the uniquely vital inner flame of the spirit, and to dissolve in it. "Not the flesh is alive, but the spirit," he proclaimed. He offered the highest truth, but not reality. He was a blind seer whose inner eye shone, but whose outer eye was veiled.

Eventually he was to see. Even at the time he caught at least a gleam of real life. It was reality when Frederician Prussia, however machinelike and artificially designed, produced men and heroes who made the heart beat faster. And Fichte could not deny their spell. "At present I know of no land, other than perhaps the Prussian territories, where at the mention of certain names powerful corollary ideas are evoked. When I hear the names of Keith, Schwerin, Winterfeldt, I become eager to know whether others are descended from them and will follow in their steps."[7] "But, of course," he added, "for the lover of mankind a melancholy feeling soon attaches to this memory, when he recalls the *purpose* for which their great deeds were done."

A new wave of German intellectual currents was needed to carry thinking men farther into the fullness of real life. It came with Romanticism, which unfolded in the last years of the 18th and the first years of the 19th century, and developed its most creative ideas in that early phase. We will never do Romanticism justice if we see it simply as a literary movement with some effects in other areas. Rather, where it had an impact at all, it affected the whole of life, not only the individual's feelings, but also his relationship to the great powers of religion, society, and the state. To be sure, Romanticism also derived to the highest extent from the individual's needs, and often escalated rapidly into pure subjectivity, which transformed all external realities into pleasures for the epicurean self. But Romanticism required the pleasures of the external world far more than did the idealistic individualism that preceded it. Romanticism was more receptive and in greater need of completion than classicism with its self-contained Promethean energy. If the classic writers boldly dissolved the world in the spirit, the younger, weaker generation of Romantics guided the spirit into the solid, material world, which it lovingly embraced. To incorporate the historical world in the widest sense, to discover the spiritual core in all its forms, now became the goal. "We sons of this century," cried Wackenroder, one of the first Romantics, "have the advantage of standing on a

---

7. Jakob von Keith (1696-1758), Curt Christoph von Schwerin (1684-1757), Hans Karl von Winterfeldt (1707-1757), Prussian generals killed in the Seven Years War.

high mountain peak with many lands and ages visible to our eyes, spread out at our feet. Let us use our good fortune, let us lovingly survey all epochs and peoples, and in their manifold feelings and creative works let us always seek the *human* qualities."

This intention to discover the world anew, as it were, to feel one's way into all its forms instead of mastering them by external measurements, was enormously productive. The flowering of philosophy, history, and linguistics in the 19th century is in great part due to the new skill of understanding even alien and irrational phenomena historically and in their own terms. Intellectuals resumed closer contact with the real world everywhere. Considered historically, the realism that characterizes the second half of the 19th century is linked by more than a thread to the ideas of early Romanticism. To be sure, its first leaders, Wackenroder, Schlegel, and Novalis, were themselves unable to advance from creative impulses to great creations. They were catalysts rather than supreme masters, they had something to offer to stronger natures, who took it up and developed it with new energy. Pure Romanticism was too soft an element; it became fully effective only when alloyed with firmer metal.

That already holds true of Romanticism's first great impact on everyday life, the renewal of Protestant Christianity, which stems above all from Schleiermacher's lectures on religion, published in 1799.[8] Here the delicate sensibility and understanding of the Romantics was united with the energy of an aspiring, ethical will, which left passive sensibility behind and sought to turn feelings into action. And just as important, Schleiermacher transferred idealistic individualism and the pantheistic concept of nature and divinity of Goethe's world from the sphere of pure intellect into the religious thought of Protestantism itself, and united them with those of its forces that were still vital and fresh. Beside remnants of orthodoxy, Pietism and rationalism were the two main directions that Schleiermacher found in Protestantism. Both still had vigor, but were in danger of losing it—Pietism by closing itself off from the world, rationalism by its dissolution of religion into sober, flat morality. Schleiermacher could make use of elements in both tendencies,

8. Friedrich Schleiermacher (1768-1834), theologian and associate of the Prussian reform party.

the inward piousness of the one and the ethical idealism of the other. He gave them greater weight through a new, more refined and individualistic emotional content, and through modern philosophy's more intellectual perception of the divine, while to those satisfied with a philosophical world view he held up the value of positive religion.

A native, naïve piousness also persisted in the mass of the North-German population. Some aspiring modernists had experienced it in their own youth, but in the course of their education had abandoned it. Now they could go one step farther and be free and pious at the same time. Schleiermacher's influence, however extensive we may believe it to have been, was not the only cause. His teachings coincided with the longing of many men and women for a more solid, positive basis for life than philosophy and appreciation of the arts alone could provide. After the Wars of Liberation this movement went even farther, led to the renewal of Pietism and orthodox Protestantism, and thus, gradually, again narrowed and became more rigid. But at the beginning of the century its character was still very different; the various elements of the new and old religiosity mingled in a multitude of individual shadings, here perhaps in mere play and gentle excitation, elsewhere already in profound struggle.

The new religious impulse was joined by a remarkable new political impetus. It, too, sprang from the needs of the spiritually awakened individual, and it, too, aimed at man's greater involvement in the real and the ethical world, at his closer links with the German nation, whose organic and historical conditions were only now beginning to be sensed. The absolutist-bureaucratic state remained as unpalatable as ever, but men were no longer satisfied with wishing for as little government as possible. Now they dreamed of a new kind of state in whose creation and preservation the individual could collaborate with his entire being, in the process further expanding and perfecting his powers. In the *Monologues* written at the end of the century, Schleiermacher asked: "Where can we find the ancient wisdom that tells us about the state? Where is the energy that citizenship, this highest form of existence, gives men; the consciousness, which all should share, of being part of its reason, imagination and strength? Where is the love for this new existence we have created?" These words announced a new level of modern individualism. Schleiermacher felt and recognized that the individual, if he lived for the whole, needed to lose nothing, but could vastly expand his personality if he merged his uniqueness with the community.

Ernst Moritz Arndt was one of those who had prayed as a boy, mocked and doubted in adolescence, and recaptured his religious feeling in maturity.[9] Like others he was painfully conscious of the lack of soul of the traditional state, which, he said, "needed only machines and was unaware that it would someday need men." He, too, longed for a new state in which basic human qualities could flower again, and more bluntly than Schleiermacher he demanded that the state be "earthy," that it be a popular and national state, bound together by the natural bonds of common language, thought, and culture. The great idea dawned in him that the nation's culture needed a firm base in the existence of people and state to remain vital and pure. "How," he asked, "can German culture exist without a vigorous popular life, which is born only of the unity of people and state? . . . As a people's political foundations disappear, all strength and striving will die. Only if we possessed a fatherland, if we possessed the supreme human and political ideas of our own united strong people, would we achieve stable customs, firm character and form, only then could the highest and most splendid human qualities grow from earthly roots into trees towering in the sun."

An abundance of such ideas flowed from his book *Germany and Europe* in 1802. We would search it in vain for practical guidelines for the constitution of a national state. It was already enough of an achievement that he recognized this state as a vague ideal, whose time would come. We should note that he did not regard the inevitably approaching national state as a force that should totally dominate the individual's existence. Even this passionate advocate of German nationhood could not deny the individualistic, cosmopolitan strain of a previous cultural epoch. "Man," he proclaimed, "should forever stand higher than the state, which cannot be allowed to shackle his powers." It is this mixture of universally human and national concerns that characterizes the new political ideas. They emerged whole from the purely cultural values that

9. Ernst Moritz Arndt (1769–1860), writer and poet, the most significant propagandist of the Prussian reform movement.

scholars and artists held, but which they came to feel were incomplete. Even as uncompromising a man as Fichte now shared this feeling. In the first years of the new century he was becoming more gentle, warmer, and allowed himself to fall under the influence of some Romantic ideas. To the extent that he was at all capable of comprehending the purely emotional, he perceived the nature of religious feeling, and he submerged his world view in its flood: "Moral man spoke of duty and commandment—what do these mean to religious man? The spiritual flowering of life, the only element in which he can breathe." If, as he believed, the ethical imperative would vanish in the heat of new religious experience, how much truer would this be of the state's imperative? Those in whose hearts the flame of heavenly love is ignited, he said, will float free and independent even above the state, no matter how shackled they might outwardly appear. But in the heightened, more positive sense of life that now filled him, Fichte also thought of the state differently than before. He no longer conceived of it simply as a menial tool for the creation of culture, nor merely as a "community of men," but as an enduring supra-individual order, which could summon all men to work for the state since its true purpose was culture itself. He did not demand a new despotism; out of love for the enduring community the citizen should freely accept the state. A harmonious stream of life would thus flow through the individual and humanity, state, culture, and religion. "Intensely human and intensely political ideas" merged in him as they did in Arndt. But Fichte was still too cosmopolitan to give his heart, as Arndt did, to the one, the hoped-for German national state. He did have Prussia in mind when in 1804, in the *Foundations of the Current Era,* he admonished states that were not naturally powerful to practice the wise art of internal reform, for the sake of political self-preservation if nothing else. But as yet he was unwilling to remain with a state that ignored his warnings and thus eventually perished: "Then let simple men, who find their fatherland in the soil, the river, the mountain, remain citizens of the fallen state—the sun-linked spirit will inevitably be drawn toward light and justice."

He still soared too far above the real world. New and traumatic experiences were needed to pull him and others like him fully down to earth. Should we wish that this had happened sooner? Should we view the whole development that has been sketched here as nothing but the prodigals' return to their father's house, and regret the long estrangement between the real state, the real nation, and this generation of giants? That would be taking too narrow a view. It would mean that we interpret German classicism as a magnificent aberration, as a blossom flowering from a diseased root. An eternal achievement needs no apologies for what it may lack. As it stands, classicism is a whole, combining elements that belong together—a unity that developed from inner necessity. Measured by its own standards, classicism's lack of political concern is certainly not transformed into an advantage, but the apolitical strain becomes an unavoidable condition for the sum of its virtues. Men needed this alienation from state and fatherland so that they could soar high into the cosmos, so that the human soul could be lifted toward the divine. There are times when all historically created intermediary forces between the human and the divine must be torn down to open the way for direct communion and make possible the discovery of new values. The path of modern man runs between highest intellectual and spiritual creation, and intense activity in the practical world. Man needs both; achievement in one area sometimes leads to greater achievement in the other. The modern sense of realism could not have worked its great transformations, had it not originally been nurtured by the spirit of the late 18th century. Man had to be freed from the constraints of reality before he could return to master and shape it. First his spirit had to expand and become supple, before he could apprehend and dominate real life in its complexity and demands. And throughout the heavy labor with harsh reality, the political, social, and economic tasks of the 19th century, the ideas of German classicism provided an inexhaustible source of intellectual and psychological rejuvenation. They arch over the 19th century much as the serene world of Platonic ideas arches over the world of the senses.

In this framework, the turn of the German spirit toward the Prussian state and the transformation of the state can be seen as the first great, epochal step, from ideas down to reality, that was taken on German soil. It is the first of the great practical achievements of 19th-century Germany, a success brought about by the forces of late 18th-century idealism. The nature and development of this idealism showed us why it was reaching out for more concrete worlds to affect. But how, we must ask again, could it be attracted to such brittle, heterogeneous material as Frederick's Prussia? How could Fichte, Wilhelm von Humboldt, and Arndt overcome the antipathy they felt toward this harsh, mechanistic state of bureaucrats and soldiers?

Their antipathy was overcome, to begin with, by the approaching peril of foreign rule. The new threats to intellectual freedom were worse than anything ever committed by the Frederician state. If Prussia had sinned by treating the mass of its subjects only as means for her ends, Napoleon used whole nations and peoples as mere raw material. Centuries of European history, the *ancien régime* no less than the revolution, seemed to have labored only to provide him with tools of power, which he adapted to his uses without concern for the particular life they contained. He undertook to transform the most inflexible among the old institutions, the Papacy and the Catholic Church, into a functional organ of his world empire; he exploited the ideals of 1789, and simultaneously stifled their love of liberty. He bent and adapted existing qualities for the purpose of power and war with a violence that surpassed anything done in this vein by Brandenburg-Prussia. Admittedly he also brought some of the blessings of the French Revolution to the conquered peoples and showed Germany impressive examples of state energy and state renewal. He smashed the decrepit features of the old era, above all the world of ecclesiastical principalities. But he also threatened viable elements, and all internal and external independence, and this aroused the more idealistic Germans against him. They felt suffocated under his ever-advancing pressure. And since only Prussia among the German states remained firm after the dissolution of the Holy Roman Empire and the defeat of Austria in 1805, their hopes now turned to her. The spring of 1806 brought the sorry spectacle of Prussia being forced against her will into the great struggle that Napoleon was waging against England. "Every noble, principled spirit in Prussia," recounts Steffens, "seemed most closely attached to England at the very time that this country was about to declare war on us." When Prussia at last roused herself to oppose the French assault on her political independence, she still fought only with the weapons of her old military system, but these were already accompanied by the wishes of Germany's poets and thinkers. Fichte wanted to march to war as an unofficial chaplain, and in June 1806 Schleiermacher wrote the memorable words: "Remember that our whole life is rooted in German freedom and German convictions, which now are at stake. Believe me, sooner or later a war will break out whose object will be our convictions, our religion and education, no less than our external freedom and possessions; a war that must be fought, but that the kings with their hired armies cannot fight, only the people together with their kings." Thus the last war of Frederician Prussia could already be seen as the first war of a new, national Prussian state.

The hopes that Prussia would be the protector of German freedom and culture would be incomprehensible had not Prussia for some time exhibited some characteristics very different from those that so pained Humboldt and Fichte. We must now complement our earlier picture of the old Prussia. We cannot do it justice unless we look beyond the state to the men who had created and maintained it. Above all we must enter into the German mind of the time and appreciate what Frederick the Great meant to his contemporaries purely as a human phenomenon. We can never ignore Goethe's testimonial to the powerful, inspiring impression of the king's personality. Here was a man greater than his work, who had struggled with destiny, not simply as a colossal, despotic ego defying fate, but as an ethical being, struggling with fundamental issues in his own breast. For the first time in many years the image of a great, truly human and humanly understandable existence appeared before German eyes, a life inextricably linked to a great political task. A great man serving the concept of the state—that meant far more than the concept itself; something new had entered the relationship between individual and state. The relationship went beyond the existing state, and men could not yet consciously understand it; but perhaps Fichte already sensed it vaguely when, in 1793, he called Frederick—largely because of his tolerance—"educator of the peoples toward freedom."

Frederick's personality and heroism had far-reaching effects. No matter how strictly we separate the man from his work, gradually his character cast a brighter light even on his state. Prussia could then appear as the personification of political energy itself, and that attracted energetic men from throughout Germany to her service. Prussia, we know, was also the state of a more liberal Protestantism. Heroism, military glory, energy, enlightened Protestantism—these were the forces that made Prussia appealing in Germany, and that brought her many of the great men who later had the task of returning Prussia to the German fold. One of the first from the Holy Roman Empire, who entered her service in 1780, while Frederick was still alive, was Karl vom Stein.. In part he was drawn by the illusion that the king would shield the old imperial German constitution against the expansionist plans of the Austrian emperor, Joseph II. Others, like Gneisenau in 1786, and Scharnhorst in 1801, were attracted by the opportunity for better careers. But misconceptions and personal considerations do not lessen the fact that Prussia already strongly attracted able men—men of action, to be sure, rather than thinkers, but only deeds could introduce new attitudes and ideas to the Prussian state, and these three—Stein, Gneisenau, and Scharnhorst—were children of the new, freer German spirit.

Of course the old Prussia as we know it could not yet give such men the scope they needed. Of them all, Stein was afforded the greatest opportunity because he joined the administration of the Westphalian provinces, where Frederick had not used the methods of the centralized state as rigorously as in the provinces of the eastern heartland. In Westphalia the institutions of the older corporative era were still preserved, and some had sufficient vitality to permit further development. That was above all true of the regular meetings of the individual administrative districts in Cleves-Mark, in which owners of "noble" estates, domain stewards, and deputies of the peasants assembled under the chairmanship of the county councilor. The assembly not only assessed and collected the taxes demanded by the state, but deliberated on the needs of the district and allocated funds to meet them. It was a modest exercise in self-government and the citizen's participation in public affairs. This and other remnants of corporative life differed somewhat from those in the eastern provinces, because they were based on unique social and economic conditions. The landed nobility meant much less in Westphalia, the middle class and peasantry much more. Nor was the demarcation between the urban and rural economy as sharp in these commercial and industrial areas. On the whole, conditions resembled those of the neighboring Netherlands, whose newer social and administrative system also developed directly from old corporate institutions, without passing through the intermediary stage of the absolutist state. As a senior official and later head of the Westphalian administration, Stein approached these local conditions and institutions with sympathy, and furthered rather than inhibited their development.

Let us return from the west to the extreme east of the monarchy, to East Prussia, where, as we have seen, Kant and Kraus inspired a new generation of officials and officers with the spirit of reform. The mood of reform, however, was awakened not only through intellectual and personal influence, but also by economic conditions. East Prussia's grain surplus, which could only be sold abroad, and her role as broker between her Slavic hinterland and international trade, drove her to favor free trade. Together with the economic theories of Adam Smith and Kraus, which were of practical benefit to the Königsberg merchants, they also adopted more liberal social and political ideas.

Finally, since 1797 some movement took place at the center of the state. The young king Frederick William III ascended the throne resolved to be a just, mild monarch to his people. He wanted to learn from the French Revolution. In a programmatic essay, written before his coronation, he said that the Revolution "provides a powerful, terrifying example to all bad rulers who, unlike good princes, do not live for the welfare of their country, but like leeches suck it dry." He was concerned for the people and in general was touched by the philanthropic spirit of the 18th century, without ever fully adopting it as his view of life. He wanted to preserve the Frederician system of government, but soften its harsher aspects and reform obvious abuses. Some men in his environment, however, wanted to go farther. His teacher Suarez, the principal author of the Prussian Law Code, had already impressed him with the demand that the wise ruler must govern over free citizens, not machines, and the cabinet councilors Mencken and Beyme, who assisted him in the first years of his reign, were ambitious to transform something of this principle into practice.[10] We know what the king's cabinet or office meant in the Prussian system. Now, in this central agency of government, humane and liberal middle-class ideas surfaced,

10. Karl Gottlieb Suarez (1746–1798), Prussian jurist; Anastasius Ludwig Mencken (1752–1801), Prussian cabinet councilor; Karl Friedrich von Beyme (1765–1838), Prussian cabinet councilor, later minister of justice.

and some Prussians already began to draw parallels with France and to speak of a party of the *tiers état* opposed to the privileged groups. The essential difference with France, of course, was that in Prussia the *tiers état* was not the party of the middle class as such, only of educated officialdom. But the high bureaucracy had now acquired self-confidence, and in 1799 a Prussian minister could say to a French visitor: "The revolution you carried out from below will in Prussia occur gradually from above . . . in a few years there will no longer be a privileged class in Prussia."

Beyme began to concern himself with the condition of the peasants. On the state domains he had a free hand, and from 1799 to 1805 important reforms were carried out. The landowning peasants on the domains of the eastern provinces were freed, if they wished, from the enforced labor that they owed the domain manager, and paid rent instead. In the process they were emancipated and gained legal possession of their farms, except in East and West Prussia, where this was not done until 1808 under Stein's administration. The radical consequentiality of France was not followed, but neither was the program stopped if, as happened, the peasants themselves did not immediately perceive the benefits of emancipation. The peasants on the royal domains could be guided by superior understanding, as though they were children of the state; between the other peasants and the state stood the landed nobility, and here the state's energy failed. The king wished to abolish hereditary servitude, gradually, without damaging the landowner. But when it came to the point, in 1803, he did not dare implement the ordinance that introduced abolition to the first province, East Prussia. He had a freer hand in another agrarian-social question; it was wholly in his power to decide whether the prohibitions that his predecessors had placed on the purchase of noble estates by the middle class should be preserved. It is indicative that he did not dare abolish the principle itself, but that in practice most such requests from bourgeois were granted.

In 1798, at the king's behest, a finance commission reporting directly to him was established, with the task of examining all branches of the administration and of proposing reforms. He himself gave the commission a promising directive by suggesting the possibility of imposing land taxes on the nobility, and in general of lifting a number of exemptions. But only a beginning was made in 1799, by depriving the nobility of some tariff exemptions it enjoyed. This was the principal, very modest result of the commission's work. The group proposed other useful reforms; it agreed with the king that the inland duties, which shut off one province from another, should be abolished. But it required Stein, who in October 1804 was appointed head of the Excise and Factory Department in the General Directory, to implement, in 1805, this essential reform for realizing the concept of a unified state—not yet universally, but with the prospect of early completion. Stein also took up the commission's idea of reducing the economic separation of town and countryside by reforming the excise, and hoped in this way to open up some of the towns' monopolies and establish workshops in rural communities, as in Westphalia. He, too, as we see, did not mean to overturn traditional institutions radically, at one blow; and the Prussia of that time could not have survived radical reformist zeal. It was momentous enough that progressive forces now existed, and that they would not be content with modest results.

Since Prussia was a military state, and its civil and military institutions were so closely integrated, the progress of civil reforms depended largely on what was done in the military realm. Again we see new ideas coming forward in the time before 1806, and the rigid structure of Frederician military institutions beginning to loosen. Thoughtful officers came to doubt the absolute value of the old linear tactics when they saw the armies of the Revolution and of Napoleon win victory after victory with new methods, in which skirmishers opened the action, shaking the enemy with aimed fire, followed by the powerful thrust of attack columns. Skirmishing was the way of fighting most closely attuned to the modern, national soldier, who could be allowed to move more freely because he is more trustworthy than the hired mercenary. It made greater demands on the soldier's personal abilities, and at the same time demanded that the service treat him more honorably and more humanely. The ascent of nation and individual simultaneously, the best of the ideals of 1789, was reflected in skirmishing, in which these ideals demonstrated their practical effectiveness.

The manner in which the Prussian army sought to catch up with the French is characteristic. Light infantry battalions were formed—twenty-four by 1806—which were trained in linear tactics as well as in skirmishing. There was even talk of training the entire third rank of the line infantry to skirmish, but nothing was done beyond training a few marksmen in every company. On the whole, this meant little progress beyond Frederick's occasional experiments with light troops. Innovation remained a loose appendage to the old.

Only a basic reform in the makeup of the army would have made it possible to go further. The unreliable foreign soldier would have to be eliminated. Events were pushing Prussia in that direction as the political changes created by the revolutionary wars closed off one foreign recruiting area after another. In their place the new provinces acquired in the partition of Poland could provide manpower, but it was just as unreliable and certainly no easier to train than the foreign mercenary. Therefore the old organization, discipline, and fighting methods were retained. But since the French national army could not fail to impress, people hit upon the idea, also based on historical precedents in Brandenburg-Prussia, of raising a national militia beside the standing army, a militia composed of discharged natives and of some of the men until then exempted from military duty. Major von dem Knesebeck, who developed this plan in 1803, proposed a force with the considerable strength of 130,000 men.[11] It was thought sufficient to authorize 50,000 men in 1805, but when war broke out the following year not a single battalion had been raised.

Once again men had tried to respond to new demands by appending something to the old. The existing system was continued; traditional and new institutions of state and society operated side by side in disregard of their heterogeneous character. The thought that a reform of head and limbs might become necessary did not occur to the veterans commanding the army. We cannot fault their rocklike trust in the Frederician system—it was the kind of innate faith that every army needs. But it was disastrous that this spirit was so constrained, that the traditional army organization was so rigid and inflexible, that progress within its framework was so difficult. Every real reform that was attempted opened perspectives toward further military and civil change, whose possibilities and

11. Karl Friedrich von dem Knesebeck (1768–1848), Prussian soldier. He supported some measures of modernization before 1806, but became a strong opponent of the reform movement.

range could hardly be calculated. General von Rüchel sensed this when he commented: "The Prussian military and political constitution is a venerable original. If one link is touched, the entire long chain shakes."[12] A vicious circle existed, in which social reforms were paralyzed by military conditions, and military reforms paralyzed by social conditions. The army could absorb the new forces of nation and individual only if at the same time Prussia transformed herself from a hierarchical, absolutist state into a national state. Conversely, political reform depended on modernization of the army.

As a rule in such situations the defensive and offensive requirements of the state, and its political ambitions, lead to progress and resolve the dilemma. For the most part the strongest impulses for genuine internal reforms come from the external situation of the state, and a vigorous foreign policy also carries new energies to the state's internal affairs. The ambitions of the great Hohenzollern rulers had transformed their peaceful dualistic state into an aggressive military monarchy. The same energetic drive for power that had motivated the Great Elector and Frederick should now have spurred their successor to apply the tools of reform more thoroughly. That would have been more faithful to his predecessors' spirit than exaggerated respect for their works. Instead, it might be said that Frederick William III returned to the peaceful traditions of the older territorial princes. At a time when the European balance of power was overthrown and the basis of every state's political existence was put in question, he wrote the following words as the first and key statement of his governmental program: "Undoubtedly a country's greatest happiness consists in continuing peace; the best policy therefore is to keep this principle in mind, to the extent that our neighbors will leave us in peace." But the Declaration of Neutrality that was embraced after the Peace of Basel of 1795 eventually became fatal to Prussia. The state withdrew from the sphere of danger, from its harsh but also healthy atmosphere, just as in the decades before the Thirty Years War men had bent low to escape the swift pace of events.

---

12. Ernst Friedrich von Rüchel (1754–1823), one of the army's senior commanders in the campaign of 1806, during which he was severely wounded. Clausewitz called him a "concentrated distillate of pure Prussianism."

A curious configuration of facts and implications resulted from these tendencies. Prussia's misfortune was not that she remained a military state, but that she remained one with obsolete means. Her misfortune was not that her politics were too energetic and aggressive, but that they had ceased to be so. If Prussia had really been a major power, she should now have reformed and allied herself with Germany's new intellectual forces. There was validity in Fichte's warning in 1804 that a state not favored by nature, a state that wished to maintain itself in the international community, should now exercise the wise art of internal modernization.

On the other hand, did we not see that the peaceful decade of 1795 to 1805 was a blessing for German intellectual life? That this very tranquility allowed German culture to produce its most splendid flowering? We are faced with a tragic contradiction, in which the desirable directions of culture and of the state cross each other, and we are reminded of the Reformation with its disastrous consequences for Germany's political existence. But the Reformation, too, eventually proved one of the deepest sources of national rebirth, and now, more rapidly than in those days, the conflict between state and culture was to dissolve in harmony. As German intellectual life was peacefully unfolding, it already began of its own accord to transform esthetic and philosophical ideals into ethical and political values; and thus halfway met the state, which wished to rejuvenate itself.

To be sure, as long as the schism between state and culture was not resolved, it directly damaged the state's internal structure. The neo-humanistic ideal included not only seeds of a creative masculinity, but also an epicurean egoism and the weak withdrawal from activity, and it was this strain that first affected the state. The mood of calm enjoyment, so damaging to the state, affected not only the king; it was nourished by the false philanthropy of his contemporaries. A remarkable change in the attitude of Prussian officials and officers can certainly be traced to this spirit of the times. A new conceit appeared, a rebelliousness against authorities until then unquestioningly obeyed, that drove the young sovereign to bitter complaints. The moral integrity of the bureaucracy also suffered; ugly scandals became known, exposed by men who enjoyed playing the judges of public morality. In the same years in which the Romantics flourished in Berlin, the capital became a site of sensual enjoyment and moral laxity. Individualism, appreciating the world and its own values, also displayed coarser, more vulgar features—as had also happened in the pleasure-seeking days of the Italian Renaissance. In the process the psychological bases of Frederick's state and army vanished—the sense of authority, the spartan frugality, the strict external discipline. The ordinances of the post-Frederician era indicate that the old, terribly severe system of discipline and punishment was no longer felt to be wholly appropriate. Some features were softened; men wished to be humane, and yet they did not dare relinquish the tools of the old system completely. To be sure, some younger officers were not only humane but also energetic; instead of relying on the old mechanical authority, they understood how to use means commensurate with an individual sense of honor. But testimony of the most reliable contemporaries shows that in general the new attitudes loosened discipline. And the glue dissolved not only in the lower echelons. Episodes in the disastrous battles of Jena and Auerstedt, and the disgraceful capitulations of fortresses that followed, testify that for the most part senior commanders, too, had lost determination and spirit. And finally, since the focus of the old institutions, the firm leadership of the commander-in-chief, was also missing, the military power of the old Prussian state crumbled like dry-rot.

The causes of Prussia's military catastrophe were therefore twofold—if we disregard Napoleon's genius and the numerical superiority of his forces. The Frederician army's organization and tactics were obsolete, and were no match for the resources of the new era, used by Napoleon. Besides, this obsolete army was no longer the force that Frederick had led; its strength had been sapped by the destructive effects of the new spirit, so that the weaknesses of the old and new era fatally converged.

Here we take leave of the old Prussia. Certainly the change to the Prussia of the reform era is not a change from night to day. We have seen that the Frederician state, even at its zenith when it contrasted most sharply with the new culture, contained some bridges and paths to the new age. We also saw that under the impact of new ideas and attitudes, the substance of Prussia did not remain unchanged. New noble as well as vulgar elements surfaced and slowly transformed, at once destructively and creatively, Prussia's inner life. Even without the catastrophe that suddenly crushed the state, these forces would have continued their work; with what result, no historical interpretation can judge. Probably matters would have taken their course more soberly, with less esthetic appeal, but they would also have lacked more than simply the drama of precipitous decline and steep ascent. The stormy acceleration of the developmental process that followed on Napoleon's victory released forces that, in a peaceful and gradual change, would probably in the main have remained latent. If the Peace of Basel was necessary to bring German culture to its purest unfolding, the tempestuous years from 1806 to 1815 were needed to give it the widest access to the German state.

CHAPTER 4

The Reformers

In the winter of 1807, Fichte delivered his *Addresses to the German Nation* in Berlin. In these lectures German philosophy descended from its heights to the people, and the proud, sovereign individual yielded to the maternal arms of the nation. "We are conquered," he called to his listeners; "the clash of weapons is ended. If we will it, a new struggle of principles, of morals, of character now begins." Under the conditions in which he spoke, the speculative thinker could offer his audience only spiritual weapons; but each lecture makes it apparent that behind the force of the spirit his visionary eye discerned the armed force of a rising generation of Germans. Thus Fichte's *Addresses* invoke the strongest metaphysical as well as the most urgent practical concerns of his age. It constituted his particular greatness that he lifted the concrete tasks of the hour into the sphere of infinity. A higher patriotism, he said, understands that the nation is the sheath of eternal qualities. In remarkable fashion he still merged fatherland and state with individual and universal human ideals. For him Germanness stood above all for intellectual achievement and a genuinely universal culture; his patriotism, it has been well said, was the twin of cosmopolitanism. With curiously rigid syllogisms and propositions that assaulted reality he sought to demonstrate that the German nation, through her language and literature above all, represented the true values of humanity. By outlining a coercive, artificial program of education for Germany's children he tried to show how the nation could be preserved. But this essentially impossible scheme was enveloped by a halo of intense, elemental feeling, which could enflame all kindred spirits. And occasionally he, too, tired of proofs, and burst out with natural simplicity: Not concepts, but immediate experience must prove that German patriotism exists and that it is of infinite value. "Whoever does not feel it, cannot be convinced."

Thus emotion swept thought from the realm of speculative reason to reality, to the state and nation. The state, Fichte now said, is the means for achieving the higher purpose of educating and developing the element of pure humanity in the nation. But while acknowledging the state as a living organ of the nation, he held up to both the higher ideal of humanity, an ideal he would not abandon. He spoke to a Prussian audience and with reference to the Prussian state, but his vision still extended far beyond immediate issues.

Even when Fichte joined the reformers of the state and the nation, he remained the philosopher, and he can be called a reformer only in a more general sense. His relationship to the men who fought to bring about concrete change was that of a chaplain to soldiers in battle. But since he associated himself with the endangered vanguard, and advanced with them, it is appropriate that a study of the leading reformers mentions him in first place.

The reformers themselves should be discussed before the reforms because the most characteristic trait of these years in Prussia is the emergence of dominant individuals in the state. Modern man now entered the political organism with the intent of conquering it. It was nothing new for men with modern attitudes to occupy positions of central authority; they were in evidence from the days of Emperor Frederick II in the Middle Ages to the Frederician age. But on the whole they had driven the state from the outside, as it were; guiding it as one would a machine. The reformers, on the contrary, wanted to possess the state, and infuse it with their blood. That was not possible without great conflicts and disappointments. But again and again new waves of individual energies pushed things forward. Men who became discouraged, stepped aside, and despaired of the state, might tomorrow rejoin it without reservations. This coming and going is characteristic of the careers of many reformers. Intense attraction between state and individual alternated with repulsion, but in the long run attraction was the stronger force. Usually, of course, whether men served in government depended on the degree of political pressure that France exerted on Prussia. But in the final analysis the movement in and out of the office was an element in the struggle these men waged for the soul of the state. They needed to perfect it for their personal happiness. The individual's most profound feelings and desires formed the base for the attempted conquest of state and nation.

Even before 1806, as we saw, intellectual developments pointed in that direction, and the reformers in their effort possessed an advantage that later generations lacked. The state they wanted, and the nation for which they lived, were not yet the relatively finished entities they are today. Much did not yet exist, but had to be created. Because the reformers were innovators their political concepts contain much that is personal and original. It is also the reason why their ideas are too much influenced by the accidents of their particular backgrounds and by outdated remnants of 18th-century rationalism. For the same reason their policies often aimed higher than the targets attainable at the time. In spite of everything, the Prussian state could not be completely transformed. When the old and dilapidated superstructure was torn down, indestructible foundations were revealed, so that in the end the new edifice again became a mere superstructure on old walls. It was a repetition of the process by which the Brandenburg-Prussian state had been created, but a repetition with an important difference. No-one in the 17th century thought of building a new state. The only changes wanted were those that would generate additional power, and anything old but still serviceable was used. The reformers' intentions went much farther. Their aim was not merely to satisfy the immediate needs of this particular state, but also to work for the rights of the individual, for the nation, and for mankind itself, for the highest cultural and personal values. The "soaring spirit" to quote Arndt, rose above the state, and it is curious and significant to see how purely political considerations now merged with unpolitical elements, or with political elements that transcended the state, and how a belief in the supremacy of the individual converged with the vital interests of the monarchy and its traditional but still viable institutions.

More than anyone else, the king saw it as his task to preserve the traditions of the old state during the process of reform. We already know that he did not possess the quality central to the Frederician concept of the state: the will for power. He wanted to preserve, not conquer. For him the state was an inheritance, which he managed with an anxious sense of duty. What he himself regarded as his highest obligation was now given further urgency and significance by the changed political situation. Between 1807 and 1812 Prussia's political future was uncertain; one had to be prepared that Napoleon would destroy Prussia if he thought it politically expedient. No doubt the king recognized that in such an eventuality his supreme duty was to fight and perish heroically, while the immediate obligation must be the internal regeneration of the crippled state. The law of political self-preservation finally made him determined to proceed to thorough reforms. But he interpreted the preservation of the state much more narrowly than did the reformers whom he now summoned. Even threadbare survival sufficed for him; he wished to delay as long as possible the time when arms would be raised in a struggle for life and death, and he clutched at the hope that the storm might, after all, pass him by. He was prepared to bear even humiliations to prolong the state's existence. He distrusted his own abilities, and therefore also distrusted the capacities of his state and his people. His pronounced critical bent and his lack of imagination preserved him from illusions, but they also denied him vision and an accurate assessment of those matters that are comprehensible only if the observer integrates individual phenomena. His inability to do so was the personal root of his timid and modest policies; the objective political root lay in the strong dynastic strain that continued to characterize his conception of the state. He regarded it a great victory if only the dynasty were preserved, and consequently accepted—though regretfully—the sacrifices of honor and independence that the state was compelled to make. It was this that distinguished him most sharply from the leading reformers. For them the preservation of this particular state and its dynasty were not supreme values. As we have already said: they soared above the state. They were not as personally rooted in the state as the king was because their thinking was less specifically Prussian and dynastic than his.

And yet, some significant points of agreement did exist between them. With his penetrating critical mind the king recognized most of the severe defects of the traditional administrative and military institutions as clearly as did the reformers. Before 1806 he had been in favor of some of the changes that were now proposed, but let the matter drop out of respect for the dignitaries who advised against them. One effect of the catastrophe, it has been pointed out, was the downfall of these false authorities, and now the king's sounder instincts came in contact with the energy and determination that he himself lacked. He permitted even far-reaching innovations, which he himself could hardly have conceived. But he also forbade other complementary reforms when made suspicious by political difficulties or by forceful protests from conservatives. The uneven, fragmentary character of the reform legislation is due in part to his character. His own political thought should not, for that reason, be termed asymmetrical and contradictory. The liberal, humane tendencies of the early years of his reign, to which he could now give freer scope, were well suited to his simple, patriarchal ideal of a "loyal, peaceful, pious, obedient people"; and he conceived of his dynastic rights in a similar paternal, moral sense. He was not a significant but a self-contained and consistent personality, whose reserve, to be sure, was based largely on a lack of receptivity. If despite his laconic, brittle ways he was able to win the respect and even love and devotion of his intellectual superiors it was largely due to his simple human virtues. Historical interpretation cannot of course end with these. Historians will always have to recognize him as the representative of a limited, but firm and tenacious concept of the state, and they will also have to admit that he was not rigidly and exclusively devoted to his views but could give scope to the great demands of his age. Only to a degree, of course; but a truly harmonious union between the overly expansive ideal of the reformers and the excessively narrow ideal of the king was scarcely possible.

Even the woman who shared his throne could not have fully succeeded in bringing about such a reconciliation, because Queen Louise was not a true political individual, despite her profound and emotional concern for the destinies of the state and its people. Her view of human beings and her dealings with leading officials were not wholly free of weakness and caprice. Still, in our discussion of the reformers we can acknowledge her mere presence as helping awaken the spirit of change and of patriotism as few others did. When the gravity of events divested her of the tinsel of court life she did not shed the delicate grace that had once beguiled all hearts, but it was now allied with moral strength and true confidence in

God. The letters in which she poured out her feelings during these years of crisis still strike a feminine note with their sudden shifts from domestic life to political affairs; the heroic passion that sometimes fills them can turn to helpless frailty. But in both moods she was honest and moving, and behind the changes we sense a strength and piety that will not yield. Since she felt herself to be a German princess as much as a Prussian queen, and since the brilliance of German artistic and intellectual life enveloped her, she was a symbol that could appeal to all, most powerfully after her frail constitution collapsed and she died in 1810.

"Where is Stein?" she had written in the depth of distress in 1807. "He is my last hope. A great heart, an encompassing mind: perhaps he knows remedies that are hidden to us." In this spirit she helped raise the greatest of Prussia's civil reformers, Karl vom Stein, to his place in history. Once he had become first minister he could hardly help but surpass her husband, and yet some affinities did exist between him and the king. If the simple, upright monarch, with his "pure love of goodness," to quote Stein, was traditional in a positive sense, Stein's ethics, too, had a traditional German coloring. In general, much of the simple, modest, religious, and moral conduct of earlier generations had survived in Protestant north Germany beneath and side by side with intellectual changes and new cultural ideals. This older layer of German life re-emerged in Stein, not in the narrow form it assumed in Frederick William, but with an elemental force that, above all, did not limit itself to private virtue. It was Stein's principal inspiration throughout his life that the wealth of moral capacity that rested in the German people should become active in public life, that the virtue of the private citizen should grow into a practical, selfless public spirit. It has often been claimed that Stein based himself on the needs of the whole community, even of the state, an interpretation that places him in opposition to the individualism of his age. But that does not accurately characterize his ideal. In Stein we never feel the "sharp, penetrating air" of the modern state, to quote Ranke, the quality that emanates from the great political realists of the modern age, that cool *raison d'état,* which acknowledges only those forces that are politically expedient and feasible, and that lead to power. His political thought was always dominated by ethical values—ideals, to be sure, that led directly to the state and could be fulfilled only by the state. But he did not think of politics primarily in terms of power and authority. To him the state meant above all a gathering of the people's ethical energies, and the supreme means for their development—"a school for building the character of man," as the historian Heinrich von Sybel once paraphrased his thought. Even in that role Stein did not regard the state as an all-powerful, all-inclusive organism. The state socialism that Fichte advocated for a time, a system that sought to bring all cultural and ethical efforts under public control—that wished to command culture, one might say— was entirely alien to him. In fact for Stein the state never becomes an abstract absolute, is never personified as it was in Greek and Roman antiquity; rather he experiences it as a living community in the old Germanic fashion. When he speaks of the state we sense that he has in mind the assembly of free German warriors. He rejected Frederician bureaucratic absolutism just as he rejected the basic individualism of Fichte and Humboldt. Unlike Humboldt he did not accuse the old state of smothering the individual, he accused it of stifling all community spirit by refusing to grant property owners a role in administration.

We can see that his basic ideas were uncomplicated and easy to grasp. When kept from serving the state, he said, the individual is driven to selfishness, pleasure-seeking, and idleness, or to arid speculation, while the state is deprived of its best resources, and is ruined by red tape, bureaucratic routine, and the indifference of its officials. His vocabulary contains few words with which to vary these statements, but they never lose their appeal, and offer nourishment and strength like good country bread. At the very time that Prussia was defeated and humiliated they rose to a level of magnificent assurance. In his "Nassau Memorial" of June 1807 he firmly stated that the administrative reforms he was advocating aimed at the "revival of sentiment for the fatherland, at independence and national honor."

As we said, he cherished neither the state for its own sake nor the sovereign individual. He was incapable of gauging the full significance of the neo-classic concept of individualism. He did not really appreciate its human values nor the effect it might have in stimulating the modern state. His passionate nature could make him bitterly unjust toward the philosophic, meditative tendencies of his contemporaries. And yet an affinity exists between this old-fashioned, stubborn, practical man and the great thinkers and poets of his time. We are reminded of the young Goethe during his years in Strassburg when we read in the "Nassau Memorial" that "a living, purposeful, creative spirit and a wealth of ideas and feelings drawn from the fullness of nature must at last replace routine and red tape." We think of Rousseau, Herder, and the many others who were seeking to return to the reality of nature. Stein's battle with the bureaucracy was undoubtedly part of the great war against everything conventional and mechanical in life that was being waged in Germany ever since the opening shots had been fired by the poets of the *storm and stress* period.[1] The revitalizing wells that Stein wanted to make available to the withered state in the practical insights of its citizens and in their participation in public affairs, were not far removed from the wells of realism and feeling that thirty years earlier the young Herder and Goethe had opened for the development of individual personality. In the 1770's the urge toward a blunt, healthy reality was more pronounced than in later decades when a more intellectual individualism dominated. At that time men rejoiced in the traditional ability and energy of the German burgher, as Stein still did. Goethe, after drinking deeply from this source, hurried on. Stein wanted to return it forever to his people.

Stein's personal development did not remain wholly unaffected by the gentle sentiments of the Werther period and the cult of Rousseau. Admittedly, he strongly rejected Rousseau's daydreaming and his "passive abandonment to outside impressions." But he could express the pleasures of friendship and a peaceful country life in words that are reminiscent of Werther, and had greater capacities to learn and was far more receptive than the harsh, violent, authoritarian qualities of his character might at first suggest. Although he despised the impassioned systematizing and the anarchy of the French Revolution, he respected its radical patriotism, and he did not hesitate to learn from the Revolution when it offered homogeneity, linked the citizen to the community, resisted state despotism, and abolished institutions that paralyzed free, responsible creativity. Basically, the French Revolution and Stein

---

1. *Sturm und Drang* is the name given to a brief, antirationalist period in German literary history, extending from the 1770's to the early 1780's. Its most significant works are Goethe's drama *Goetz von Berlichingen* (1773), his novel *The Sorrows of Werther* (1774), and Schiller's drama *Die Räuber* (1777).

faced the same challenge of reuniting state, nation, and individual. The difference was that he approached his task with greater simplicity and realism, but also with a more highly developed ethical sense, that he was not led by theories or by a crude drive for power, but by ethical concepts nurtured by his practical experiences and his sense of the past. More firmly than the French Revolution he based himself on natural development, present reality, and history.

To the extent that he used historical forces he transformed them into contemporary terms. He did not simply want to conserve the remnants of the Estates, to which he linked his ideas of self-government, because that would have meant preserving their spirit of privilege. He wanted to restructure them in a way that would foreclose a new class egotism. Nor did he wish to rejuvenate the greatest historical force that inspired him, the old German Empire, with antiquarian accuracy, but as a free recreation that would make it a strong vessel for its moral values. He did not want to cling to the past—if he nevertheless sometimes did, giving way to the power of tradition and of his sense of being descended from sovereign imperial knights, it only reveals him as one of those naïve beings who create from rich unconscious inner resources.

Other fissures existed in his thought and in his character. There were hidden depths in him, which the turmoil of the age might momentarily reveal. We shall return to some of these. For the time being it is important to recognize the unified and constant qualities of his nature, to listen not to the sudden gasps but to the calm, deep breathing of his spirit.

He was never a specifically Prussian statesman. He was not a native, and would not become part of Prussian society because he wanted to pursue universally ethical policies rather than policies of self-interest, *Realpolitik,* for which he was ill suited. Karl August von Hardenberg, who was to continue Stein's reform program, was not native to Prussia either, but his flexible spirit had the gift of adapting itself to the most varied ideas and interests. No one place could fully claim him, but he was at home everywhere, as minister of the *ancien régime* in Prussia no less than as statesman of the era of reform, and later in 1819, as the man under whom the Reaction arrived in Prussia. As reformer he could at one moment play the doctrinaire idealist, who sought to construct and follow the grand design, and at the next moment grasp only measures that were expedient. Today he would face the desperate struggle for existence with verve and pathos, only to duck smoothly and accept humiliation tomorrow. "The chancellor is governed by the all-powerful hours," said a clever woman who knew him, and Niebuhr declared bluntly that if Hardenberg threw someone down the stairs he would let the man climb back through the window the next day.[2] In 1807, when he took up the idea of reform, his slogan was "democratic principles in a monarchic government." Even more than Stein he drew on the innovations of victorious France, but with a markedly different tendency. Stein adopted those elements that created a moral bond between state and citizen, and that placed the energies of the autonomous individual at the disposal of the state. Hardenberg was certainly not unreceptive to this idea either, but in his mind, almost unintentionally, state and citizen again diverged. He wanted to offer the citizen equality and the most far-reaching freedom in civil life, especially in the economic realm: "Everyone should act according to his natural tendency in the state." He recognized that energy freely applied in trade and commerce would create more goods than did constant bureaucratic tutelage, and in the final analysis would bring greater benefit to the state. He removed the bonds because it was good for the state, and also because he liked to give men freedom. As a benevolent epicurean who lived and let live it pleased him to give anything at all. But with the same ease he accustomed himself to the equally "natural tendency" of the state toward power and the increase of power, and he did not seek this increase solely or even mainly in the alliance of state and people. He placed at least as much value on increasing the power of government by means of administrative efficiency. Consequently he relieved the bureaucracy of some of the burdens under which it had labored in the 18th century, but he held firmly to the rest and had no intention of sharing it with the governed. He would be glad to institute a nation-wide representative assembly, but one that was politically impotent and as harmless as possible. Not only the individual in his realm but also the state in its sphere should exert

2. Barthold Georg Niebuhr (1776-1831), historian, Prussian civil servant and diplomat.

the laissez-faire right of the free employment of all energies. If appropriate boundaries were observed this might constitute a convenient and acceptable coexistence; but surely not the vital cooperation of state and people envisioned by Stein.

In short, Hardenberg's thought was eclectic. The traditions of enlightened absolutism, the philosophy of the Enlightenment itself, the liberal and democratic demands of the age, the models of the Napoleonic empire and of the kingdom of Westphalia, where the new rights of freedom and equality coexisted with a tautly centralized administration and a shadowy popular assembly—all these touched him, and he had learned from everything. He was the most cosmopolitan of the reformers, in the sense that he did not completely belong anywhere, spoke a variety of intellectual and political tongues, learned and relearned easily, but, to be sure, also found it easy to forget. But for that very reason this accommodating man could in many ways adapt more closely and effectively to specifically Prussian interests than did Stein and other reformers whose ideals went beyond the mere maintenance and growth of Prussian power. During the stormy years between 1807 and 1813 Stein, who felt more German than Prussian, more the patriot than the politician, could never have steered a narrowly Prussian course in foreign policy, which sought the preservation of the state above all else. Hardenberg could; it was this fact that united him most closely with the king and formed the basis of his position of trust. Indeed, in his ambitions for Prussia, which were of Frederician cast, he far surpassed the king. These ambitions, however, were not deeply rooted either; in crises they often collapsed.

But no one was better suited to mediate between king and reformers than a man who was as expert at untying knots and removing obstacles as the pleasant, compliant chancellor. If his domestic and foreign policies lacked the powerful accents of Stein's leadership, they ran more smoothly and easily, and even were energetic whenever he felt he could take the chance. It was given to neither man to complete his work, but for Hardenberg completion was psychologically impossible.

Wilhelm von Humboldt, the third leader of the civil reforms whom we must characterize, thought of the state in terms that differed from those of both Hardenberg and Stein. In 1809 and 1810 he directed the section on culture and education in the Ministry of the Interior, and as *de facto* minister of culture was responsible for areas that perfectly suited his preferences and abilities. But they were also areas of special sensitivity in the relationship of state and individual. In earlier years he had withdrawn in pain from these contacts; he had firmly rejected any state intervention, no matter how benevolent, in the intellectual development of the individual or in the cultural life of the nation as a whole. Was he now untrue to his principles if he drafted laws for elementary and higher education, censorship directives, regulations for art academies and for the advancement of church music? He still believed government could do little to help science and the humanities: "The state," he said in 1810, "must always recognize that it does not really bring about [culture], and cannot bring it about, that—on the contrary— the state obstructs as soon as it intervenes, that basically things would go much better without the state." He justified intervention with the argument that every activity that sought to affect society needed institutions and funds. The state was obliged to provide these, but the fewer demands it made in fulfilling this duty the better. We can see that his basic views had not changed. In its relationship to letters and science he continued to regard govern- ment as a necessary evil. But gradually he was attracted to another aspect of the state. He became ambitious to be a creative statesman. The goal of true political action he now said was to make it pos- sible for ideas to put their stamp on reality. The urge to bring principles and concepts into the everyday world and to shape life in their image won him over. He learned to value the state not as the philosopher who remained captive to the ideas of his youth, but as the mature man active in political life.

It was the heightening of modern individualism, which we first perceived in Schleiermacher, that turned Humboldt into a politician, his recognition that working for the community afforded men new opportunities for personal development and effectiveness. The link of motives is significant. Once again they confirm our general observation that Germany's loftiest minds were drawn down to the state by their yearning for reality and pulsating life. It is equally evident that Humboldt, like others, was driven by his own very personal needs. But he did not renounce earlier ideals. Rather he approached the state head held high, like someone who joins the command of an army that until recently he had opposed. The autonomous, creative individual entered state service because a promising sphere of activity was opened to it and to the new ideal of German intellectual life, which can no longer be described in terms of "knowledge and talking," but of "character and doing."

This new alliance also changed the state. The rigid, blind mechanism that once had so oppressed Humboldt unfolded into the policies of the new men who worked through the machinery. They personalized the impersonal element of the state. We shall not ask whether it was possible to soften the rigid structure permanently, nor shall we examine whether Humboldt himself always acted freely, according to his personal convictions, unencumbered by the disruptive traditions of government. Sufficient that it was possible for someone like him to be in government, and that in significant issues he could put the stamp of his thought on reality. No matter how brief his term of office—that it occurred at all, that Humboldt and the Prussian state could tolerate each other for a time, is perhaps the best measure of the state's transformation.

It also indicates a change in Humboldt. The change should not be overestimated, to be sure. Even as Prussian privy councilor he remained a citizen of the world, who wanted to serve the highest values of mankind. "Nothing about a senior official," he said at the time, "is as important as his view of humanity in all its aspects, as his concepts of human dignity and human ideals." But cosmopolitanism and love of one's native land need not be mutually exclusive. We may assume that not only the longing for personal fulfillment through political activity led him to serve Prussia; he must also have been affected by the childlike, human emotion of love for his unfortunate country. A simple patriotism, which in the years of French rule could grip every German, also entered his rich and elevated spirit. Henceforth it permeated his actions, even if he made few words about it. His reflective mind shied from searching out the primitive, naïve forces in human nature; but although deeply hidden, they existed in him as in other men.

It is difficult to picture him clearly. His obvious characteristics were not what was most significant in him. He could appear cold, heartless, ironic, and superior; more robust associates said that in discussion he whittled clubs into toothpicks. His style simply was not muscular, and although he did not lack passion, even when he acted it was too refined to turn into crude political energy. He tended to step aside in high-minded renunciation, when he should have attacked. To some observers he appears as a ray of pure light passing through Prussian history; to others a bloodless shadow, or a hybrid whose ideas clashed with his actions. But those who approach him with sympathy will find him consistent and genuinely warm, and they will value the clarity with which his mind and character illuminates the eternal—and in his day central—problem of the relationship between individual and state.

Even men who were more energetic and masterful than Humboldt had to struggle with this problem, and found it impossible to serve the state without conflict. We refer to the soldiers who reorganized the army and led it to victory. At first sight they appear in a halo of national fame, men who aroused popular imagination, enthusiasm, and gratitude as the saviors and liberators of the country, heroes of countless tales in school and home, models of manliness. No people can do without such hero worship, and there must always be historians who, like epic poets, know how to renew the heroic image and satisfy the original need that is expressed in all of history. But our task is different. We seek the agitated inner life behind the armor and trophies, the threads that link the personalities of these individuals to great historical movements; we want to conceptualize the manner in which they personified those forces in German history that were pointing toward the modern state and nation.

Without exception they were not only fighters but also thinkers. Their leader, Gerhard von Scharnhorst, was even called an intellectual pure and simple, and a highly impractical one at that, a schoolmaster without strength and vitality. He could give that impression even to men who did not hate him because he had destroyed the institutions of the old army. He was, in fact, an opaque personality like Humboldt, whose best qualities were not revealed to the casual observer, who was too fully engaged with the wealth of his ideas to be easily understood. Like Humboldt he appeared vague and hazy; in reality both possessed powerful emotions and intellects, but they lacked the ordinary egotism of insisting on always making their weight felt. In the final analysis his achievements speak for Scharnhorst: he is the quiet hero of those years, the tenacious, inflexible, secretive armorer, whose work alone made the Wars of Liberation possible.

To his friends and pupils he meant infinitely more. "People like to compare me to him," Gneisenau once said; "but I am a pigmy beside this giant, whose mind I can only admire, never fully comprehend." Gneisenau did himself an injustice with this comment, and it may also have been misleading about his friend. Scharnhorst's greatness lay not in the profundity and originality of his ideas, but in their inexhaustible, steady force; their calm, sustained penetration of reality. He was the true empiricist among the reformers. He sank his plumb line most deeply into experience, and he never tired of studying reality in order to uncover the truths of practical life. Naturally his empiricism was shaped by the tendencies of his age, which liked to search for ultimate causes beneath the surface of phenomena. But if he, like his contemporaries, was never satisfied until he reached the realm of abstraction, he was more thorough and deliberate. As Arndt said of him: he did not restlessly chase ideas, but settled on them. The resting lion that adorns his tomb in Berlin is an apt symbol of his nature. Heavy, sated by experience and reflection, but always ready to spring, the Hanoverian peasant boy achieved greatness.

The major experience of his life, which he never ceased to study and turn to practical use, was the transformation of warfare by the French Revolution. When the Revolutionary wars broke out he did not immediately succumb to the new fashion that demanded the abolition of standing armies and their replacement by the people in arms. He had to see the new forces in action before he could believe in them. The campaigns of the old monarchies against revolutionary France, in which he personally distinguished himself as an officer in the Hanoverian service, showed him the frailties of traditional military institutions and the promising future of national armies. Step by step he worked his way to an understanding of the new conditions, and gradually arrived at firm concepts on reforms in all areas of war, from details of drill and discipline to the loftiest intellectual and psychological factors that determine victory and defeat. He was a gunner, that is, he belonged to a branch of the service where more than in others theory and practice are continually combined, and great effects are achieved by paying close attention to detail. Even as reformer Scharnhorst remained cautious and deliberate. He held fast to the vital elements of the standing armies, their discipline, sense of honor, and *esprit de corps,* while rejecting the deadwood, their mechanical tactics and artificial strategy, their reduction of the warrior to an automaton. To gain victory, Scharnhorst said, the soldier must again become a warrior, that is, he must infuse his actions with personal convictions, and that was possible only if he felt himself to be part of his people, and if the people as a whole became a reservoir of military strength.

In his intellectual journey from standing army to national army, Scharnhorst finally arrived at the nation itself, and its links to the state and to the individual. But it would be wrong to discuss only the progress and working of his mind. In Scharnhorst the military intellectual always contained a passionate human being, who had experienced a Werther period of his own, a time when, in his words, "nothing matters but the heart and one's basic passions; when all other concerns of life are ignored." Even this great empiricist required the experience of total emotion before he could formulate the remarkable statement of 1807 in which his spirit cast a clear light on the sufferings of the German people: "Who would not risk everything to plant the seed of a new tree, who would not gladly die if he could hope that the fruit would ripen with new strength and vitality. But only one thing can make that possible. We must kindle a sense of independence in the nation; we must enable the nation to understand itself and to take up its own affairs; only then will the nation acquire self-respect and compel the respect of others. To work towards that goal is all we can do. To destroy the old forms, remove the ties of prejudice, guide and nurture our revival without inhibiting its free growth—our work cannot go further than that."

It is not irrelevant to add that on the eve of the Wars of Liberation this profound, idealistic patriot once more fell in love—with a young, simple girl, his grandchild's governess, to whom he wrote that nothing in the world mattered to him but her love. A few months later, in May 1813, after he had been fatally wounded at Grossgörschen, he wrote to his daughter: "I want nothing from the world. What I prize I won't be given in any case. . . . I would exchange my seven decorations and my life to command the army for one day." In such passionate contradictions his life ebbed away. But unless one is aware of these passions one does not fully understand the forces of the age. Beyond the ideals of state and nation for which men were ready to die, the restless heart continued to demand its inalienable rights as insistently as it had in the days of Goethe's youth. Had men not lived so passionately they would not have been so impassioned by impersonal ideals, to which they surrendered just because these ideals held out the promise of happiness. Their clamoring heart sought fulfillment in policy and service as well as in personal relationships.

These soldiers of the reform era were a race apart. "Few men," Steffens observed in his memoirs, "had a greater opportunity for personal development in a variety of circumstances and challenges than the gifted and enterprising Prussian officers of those days. It was [in the years of reform] that their intelligence and authority acquired the strength that later enabled them to defeat the enemy." On a lesser scale the spectacle of the French revolutionary wars was repeated in Prussia, with young soldiers winning glory and marshal batons. Even the officer corps of the strictly drilled Frederician army had retained an adventurous element from earlier days, a free, wild force, pursuing war and fortune, which Frederick pruned and controlled but neither could nor wanted to eradicate. A more refined branch was grafted to this martial trunk when officers in peacetime garrisons began to seek enlightenment and self-improvement in the works of German poets and philosophers. One of these officers was Neidhardt von Gneisenau, himself a soldier of fortune, nearly abandoned at birth, moving from land to land in his youth, but early on touched by the muses. He could express his feelings and the experiences gained during an eventful life in words of remarkable beauty, which made the commonplace sound noble, the tender strong, and the passionate majestic. Like another Goethe or Beethoven, he can still move us today. On contemporaries his effect was magical because his physical appearance harmonized with his emotions and intellect. He was handsome, masculine, possessed of an unselfconscious nobility: "Everything about him seemed necessary and right." This simple statement of his friend Amalie von Beguelin identified what may have been his most characteristic quality, an aristocracy of the spirit that radiated as naturally as the sun.[3] He lacked the cutting wit and irony by which many of the most distinguished commanders of the age impressed, but also repelled, their contemporaries. After he gained the heights of success Gneisenau became if anything more modest and gentle.

---

3. Amalie von Beguelin (1778-1849), wife of a senior official in the Prussian finance ministry.

When two epochs are in conflict, men sometimes emerge who belong more to one period than to the other, and yet combine dominant characteristics of both and resolve their dissonance in harmony. Gneisenau was such a man. Originally, as we said, he was a soldier of fortune, like many poor nobles and officers of the *ancien régime*; but he became marshal of a nation-state. He himself helped to create the new state; but despite his passionate involvement he remained a citizen of the world in the Enlightenment sense. He was at once an aristocrat and democratic; servant of a prince, but in some respects a revolutionary. He could speak of the "magic" with which the "rulers of this earth" could invest their friendly words or their anger. "How many among us," he told Frederick William in the crisis year of 1811, "who are pained to see the throne tremble, might find a peaceful, happy existence in some isolated valley . . . but ties of birth, of affection, of gratitude bind us to our prince. With him we will live or succumb." He regarded these feelings as poetry of the most elevated kind: "Religion, prayer, love of the ruler, of the fatherland, love of virtue—what are these but poetry? The spirit can never be liberated without poetry."

If we consider his ideas and their historical bases in detail we gain a broad view of the emotional and intellectual landscape of 18th-century Germany. Its most varied aspects, from patriarchal sentiment to Wertherian sensibility, are combined in Gneisenau; even the trivial and sentimental, which the German Enlightenment possessed in good measure, reappears in more spiritualized and refined form. But the fervent and seemingly unconditional devotion to the sovereign, which Gneisenau justified by appealing to religion and poetry, because of that very justification constituted the allegiance of the free individual, of the man of the 18th century, to whom devotion did not imply loss of liberty. In 1813 and later, Gneisenau was to assert his sovereignty emphatically against the old dynasties; but even when he still felt himself to be their loyal servant he took up weapons that, he conceded, were borrowed from the "arsenal of the revolution." As few other Prussian reformers, he admired the French Revolution in statements that some historians have used to demonstrate the influence of the revolution on the Prussian reforms.

But Gneisenau confronted the ideas of the French Revolution with a similar sense of autonomy. He was not captivated by its theories.

Like Scharnhorst he valued, above all, the enormous energy that the revolution had generated—in his opinion primarily by giving opportunities to strong, talented men, to the "genius of common origin." This was his message when he held up victorious France as an example to Prussia: "What infinite powers slumber in the bosom of the nation, undeveloped and unused! Thousands and thousands of men possess genius, but their wings are paralyzed by the constraints of their existence. While an empire perishes in weakness and shame, its most wretched village may contain a Caesar, following his plow, or an Epaminondas, eking out his livelihood by the sweat of his brow." He painted his own past with these words. Before 1806 his wings, too, had been paralyzed, and he had suffered deeply under the constraints of his existence. Out of personal longings he developed his demands for all of society.

Each of the great reformers possessed concerns unique to himself, which formed the strongest, most personal motive for his actions. Each, basically, attempted to universalize himself. Gneisenau did this by demanding freer flight for all who were capable of it.

This explains the intense, passionate sympathy with which he followed the course of Napoleon, whom he called the greatest man of a great people, and his own teacher in war and politics. He hated him as the suppressor of liberty, but admired him as the power that had grown from liberty's soil. He hoped for an anti-Bonaparte to confront Bonaparte, his equal in strength, and like him a soldier of fortune and freedom, who emerged from the people to release and guide all its energies. The tyrant, he said in 1808, must be opposed with his own weapons, with determined men as leaders. Such statements reveal his own yearning, the beat of his heart anticipating the future. The year before, on a smaller stage, when he defended the town of Kolberg, he had discovered in himself the inexhaustible resources of the true leader; the wars of 1813 to 1815 were to carry him to the peak as the one commander in the allied camp who was Napoleon's equal.

He possessed tendencies that might have carried him even farther on the road that Napoleon had traveled. In the summer of 1813 his friend Amalie von Beguelin asked: "If he were to have the same success as Napoleon, would he be much better than Napoleon in twenty years?" She thought she perceived immense ambitions in him that might overshadow the great ideas by which he was inspired; and it may be true that Gneisenau seemed to wear an invisible crown. But even in those years of change and opportunity enough barriers remained in Germany and Prussia to thwart the ambitions of a powerful upstart. And Gneisenau was man enough to limit himself and seek his goals in the ethical and cultural ideals of the German people. He could propose the boldest, most radical means for regaining German independence, but the tempest was to be followed by the blessings of a free national existence and genuine harmony between peoples and rulers. He could dream of war and peace simultaneously, because here as there he was in his element. It was this that distinguished him most sharply from his great antagonist, who could breathe only in the atmosphere of war. While Napoleon employed the power that the Revolution had awakened in France solely as a means to satisfy the needs of his enormous ego, and served the national interest only to the extent that his ambitions required, Gneisenau, seen historically, was the champion of un-fettered individuality and free nationhood. He cherished the ideal that the same country in which religious freedom had emerged during the Reformation could now generate political freedom linked to higher social and cultural values, and that the Prussian dynasty and state were the carriers of this change. His dreams were more human than political, more German than Prussian, and his views on political and constitutional issues had more brilliance than substance. Prussia was not his native state, but rather, as he once put it with unconscious significance, the fatherland he had "selec-ted." When the Prussian state seemed to become unfaithful to its task in 1812, Gneisenau felt free to consider, with Fichtean cos-mopolitanism, transferring his allegiance to England, the country where light and justice endured. Stronger and more natural than his Prussian loyalties were his feelings for Germany; this too re-veals his intellectual roots in the 18th century. In his thought as in the thought of others, the "soaring spirit" rose above the limits of state and even of nation, but destiny and his own conscience bound his energies to Prussia. Both freedom and self-restraint were necessary to give his historical achievement its unique luminous greatness.

By following his artless genius Gneisenau made his way unreflec-tively between personal autonomy and the demands of the state. Carl von Clausewitz chose his course in a different manner. The great theorist of war was Scharnhorst's and Gneisenau's most understanding friend and ally in these years. Chance kept him in positions that limited his participation in the reforms and the later campaigns, but he became the teacher who transmitted the military heritage of the era to succeeding generations, and whose writings formed the German commanders of the wars of unification. Their tautness and intensity, fire and reserve, their rational boldness can already be found in him. He is by far the most modern of the reformers, although his intellectual world, like theirs, still bears unmistakable traits of neo-classicism and the Enlightenment. His ideas firmly bridge the philosophic spirit of the 18th century, which penetrates the appearance of phenomena to reach their intellectual base, and the realism of the 19th century, which seeks to replace assumptions with effective, decisive forces.

Clausewitz's sharp dialectical mind had been schooled in the philosophic writings of his age; from them he acquired his fearless critical faculty, his constructive sense for interconnections and patterns, and his awareness that the mind shaped reality. But while contemporary philosophy always remained more concerned with the creative spirit than with created reality, his thinking was directed toward reality from the start. He sought the facts of his world. His judgments on politics and society, on individual and national character, and especially on war, are decisive probes of a firm and creative mind. His realism preserved him from the illusions of the model-building theorist, his philosophic spirit from the short-sightedness and superficiality of men who acknowledged only what they could see with their own eyes. Everything he touched was purified in the fire of an unusually proud personality, marked by ambition and a simultaneous readiness for self-sacrifice. In clear recognition of the consequences he scaled down his ideals. From his former cosmopolitan breadth and belief in individual autonomy he crossed to the narrower world of the state and nation. It always seems selfish to me, he wrote in 1807, that a man so prides himself on his worth as human being as to become indifferent to his value as citizen. He proclaimed the fatherland and national honor as the two earthly deities he must serve, even though he knew that this elevation also implied a loss. When he compared Germans with Frenchmen he observed that the latter were superior citizens and more useful to the political leadership because they were less individualistic, more uniform, whereas their higher aspirations made Germans strain against the fetters of the state. He knew as well that the state could not exist merely to further virtue and reason, but that any political organism depended on the prejudices, passions, and even weaknesses of men. Some of Clausewitz's contemporaries, who renounced the life of contemplation and creativity and like him turned to the state, would have hesitated had they recognized as clearly as he did that the state was not always beautiful and pure. But such ambiguities did not repel a man who knew that in reality spirit and matter can never be separated. Without illusion he dedicated himself to the state, but not without passion—for he was capable not only of thought but also of hate and love.

He hated the foreign domination of Prussia, and clung to her with a deep, elemental love. In the present crisis he regarded it as everyone's inescapable, primary duty to devote all energies to her salvation. His decision to subordinate the autonomy of the individual to the duties of the citizen was both "highly human and highly political," to revert to Arndt's terminology once more. The decision is historically significant and instructive because Clausewitz reached it only with great inner turmoil. With open eyes he sacrificed the ideal of individual autonomy, in the clear light of reason he entrusted himself to more powerful, primal impulses, which bound him to his native soil, his countrymen, and to the state handed down by generations.

Clausewitz bound himself to Prussia more firmly, with less ambiguity than did Stein, Gneisenau, and Scharnhorst. It made a difference that they were newcomers while he was a native. And yet even he, understandably, could not limit himself to one land. He believed that to fight for Prussia at this juncture also was to fight for Germany and Europe. The duty evoked by the word "German," he said, was greater and more sacred than the obligation of simply preserving Prussia's existence, and when the two duties collided in 1812 he acted logically by transferring to the Russian service. In the final test, his ideals, too, ignored the boundaries of the state.

One man among the reformers did seek his salvation solely in Prussia and tied himself completely to her: Hermann von Boyen, Scharnhorst's collaborator in reforming the army, the king's military advisor during the crisis of 1811, later minister of war, and the organizer of universal conscription in Prussia. Even as a young officer in East Prussia, the "quiet, firm, modest man," as Arndt called him, believed that he could combine loyalty to Frederick and to the Prussian state with the new doctrine of moral autonomy that he had absorbed from Kant's lectures and writings. He was able to do so because freedom to him was inseparable from commitment to society and culture as a whole. He regarded the state as an educator toward freedom, particularly the Prussian state, which he believed was founded on the principles of intellectual vitality and religious tolerance. Neo-humanism and Prussian loyalties were intimately combined in these beliefs. The barbaric features of Frederician institutions did not shake Boyen's faith. He never rebelled against the state, even in his thoughts, because he was confident that humanity was steadily progressing and that sooner or later darkness would give way to light. This assurance, which he derived from the optimistic rationalism of the 18th century, obliged him to work for the great cause of ennobling the state and the citizen. Boyen, the philosopher, who wanted to regulate all aspects of society and administration according to his principles, and could choose strangely impractical methods for doing so, was also an untiring worker and a fearless fighter. He might have lacked the elemental passions and rich complexities that marked some of his greater friends, but no one surpassed him in the intensive blending of ethical ideals and political objectives, and in the firm enthusiasm with which he served both.

Boyen never ceased in his efforts to replace force, mechanical authority, and selfishness with justice, cooperation, honor, patriotism, and charity as the mainsprings in the relationship between state and citizen. But he did so without sentimentality. He wanted a strong, independent Prussia, and he defended her interests in Germany and Europe with a robust, realistic egotism, which he could reconcile with his ethical principles because he interpreted the rise and fall of states and their achievement of greater power as an outcome of their moral and psychological resources. He regarded all states as living organisms, which had to carry out their specific ethical tasks within the development of mankind. It is admirable to see how wholeheartedly he championed what he regarded as Prussia's fundamental values, and how his interpretation of her mission came to color nearly all his words and actions. There is no room in his conceptions for any conflict between power and spirit, between the state, mankind, and the individual. In Boyen's thinking the spirit soared beyond the state only in the sense that he idealized Prussia and expected too much from her.

The reformers, in short, were not uniform in ideals and outlook. The variety among them is striking, as is the wealth of ideas and ideals they now poured into the state, a vessel that evidently was too small to contain all these riches. It was not possible for such forceful and original personalities to accede totally to the special needs and assumptions of the state. Nor was it possible for the state to divest itself completely of its own past, and to adopt ideas that had little to do with state power and that had developed outside Prussia. As we know, many reformers were not Prussian. In the years of reform the old, native nobility of Brandenburg, Pomerania, and East Prussia, which had provided Frederick with most of his officials and officers, played an insignificant role. Boyen and Clausewitz were Prussian, but they came from obscure families that only recently had entered government service. They did not belong to the old, established native nobility, and that is also true of the Humboldts.

It was to be expected that the traditional elites, which had once fought king and central government to preserve their local independence, would also oppose this new invasion of alien, non-Prussian innovators. But the link between the new cultural and political ideas and the state, a link that men now tried to forge, would in any case have remained imperfect because neither of the two sides could deny its innate nature. That is why the history of the Prussian reforms is an account of partial and often contradictory political and administrative change. To understand why this was so it is not enough to say that all achievement is fragmentary. We must recognize that the ultimate, but also the most difficult, task of modern civilization is to reconcile the inalienable rights of the individual and the ethical and intellectual ideas of mankind with the harsh demands of the state, which is a self-centered, authoritarian entity. At the beginning of the great revolution when France tried to solve this problem by subordinating the state to the postulates of the rights of man, she soon experienced a terrible reaction; a far more despotic state than the monarchy of the *ancien régime* arose and largely destroyed the ideals of 1789. The Prussian reforms also suffered reverses; but perhaps the interaction of ideas and power was more intensive and proved more durable because neither side was able to overcome the other, even temporarily. Two strong forces were in conflict; neither triumphed completely, but each absorbed enough of the other and drew strength from its borrowings to provide a basis for future efforts of reconciliation. The specific issues and phases of their conflict are discussed in the next chapter.

CHAPTER 5

The Reforms

When the reconstruction of the state began after the disasters of 1806 and 1807, there were no political parties in the country that might have worked out, recommended, and pushed through a program of reform. The intellectual movement that flowed toward the Prussian state before and after 1806 was led by thinkers, not party chairmen, and they offered ideals, not legislative proposals. As had been true of Frederician Prussia, laws were drafted by senior officials and officers to whom the king had assigned this task; the acceptance of their proposals depended entirely on his will. The reform of the state was carried out by agents of the monarch, with the methods of absolutism: by bureaucratic actions sanctioned by the king.

But as we know, the officials who now advised the king were more than bureaucratic servants. Their loyalty belonged not only to the Prussian state but also to German culture, whose ideals they had made their own. That was certainly not why the king appointed them in place of his traditionalist advisors after the catastrophe; he called the new men because they seemed to have energy and strength. They showed greater determination to preserve Prussia's honor, and in general their superior talents became evident in these times of trial. As early as November 1806, only a few weeks after the defeats of Jena and Auerstedt, Frederick William offered the ministry of foreign affairs to Stein, whom he called a "mind capable of great conceptions," the man who at that very time boldly urged continuing the war against Napoleon on the side of Russia. But Stein posed conditions that showed that the king could no longer dispose automatically over such men. They harbored political demands of their own, with which the absolutist monarchy had to come to terms.

Stein demanded the replacement of cabinet government by a ministerial system. He wanted the Council of Ministers to work directly with the king so that major decisions were no longer made in the monarch's office but in council. It is no exaggeration to regard Stein's proposals as a revolt of the senior bureaucracy against the autocratic absolutism in power until then, as a preparation for the eventual transition from the absolute to the constitutional monarchy. In their present condition, Stein declared, the ministers lacked independence, and their sense of honor and responsibility was suppressed. He objected to this political tutelage, and as a first step insisted on what might be called the emancipation of the state's senior administrative officers.

Stein's demands were unheard-of in the old Prussian scheme of things, as was his rejection of the partial concessions offered by the king. As an "obstinate, defiant, stubborn, and disobedient servant of the state," the king dismissed him in January 1807. But Stein's reputation was already so considerable that the king recalled him after the Peace of Tilsit—oddly enough, Napoleon also recommended him—and named him to head the administration. On 1 October 1807 he reported to the king in Memel. His ministry lasted little more than a year, only until 24 November 1808; but this one year nurtured all of Prussian and German history in the 19th century. From this creative period institutions and attitudes emerged that continue to be alive and effective today.

And yet Stein did not nearly achieve all he set out to do. The changes brought about were not due to him alone, and some of them soon needed improvement. But achievements and individuals may be significant beyond their immediate impact; some fragments can exert strong, lasting and comprehensive influence without ever being more than fragments. Stein's legislation had epochal significance if only by proving that the Frederician state, despite its peculiar and artificial structure, and despite the enormous reduction of its political power and the loss of half of its territory, remained a vigorous organism, which could be rejuvenated, and developed in new directions. It is true that some of the loss meant little more than shedding ballast. The Peace of Tilsit deprived Prussia of her heterogeneous Polish acquisitions, "South Prussia" and "New East Prussia," while the territory she retained consisted almost wholly of her old core provinces. But how weak was her position in Europe! How ravaged was her army, once the strongest organ of the state! The military disaster had struck down the institution on which Prussia rested and which throughout the 18th century was the object of her greatest concern. If it nevertheless proved possible to create a new and different basis for the state, it was because beneath all military and civil organization lay a deeper, ideological foundation, which supported the state and enabled it to absorb innovation. To put it differently, even Frederick William I and his son had achieved more than becomes immediately apparent in their institutions. They created the beginnings of a true Prussian *nation,* and on these beginnings Stein could build further.

Stein's reforms aimed at emancipating the nation's potential energies from the shackles of bureaucratic absolutism, and teaching them to work freely for the common good. Even his reform of the central administrative agencies had this aim. If he could turn the departmental ministers of the Frederician system into independent, responsible statesmen, they would no longer act only as agents of the king but also as representatives of the community, the nation. Judged by the standards of immediate success, Stein achieved even this first among his major demands only in part. He ended the power of the cabinet councilors, but his hope that the king would now govern in collaboration with the Council of Ministers foundered on Frederick William's character. The king simply lacked the personal qualities necessary for ruling "in council" and instinctively sought a strong shoulder to lean on. Consequently a dominant first minister emerged—Stein. After Stein's departure, and after the brief ministry of Count Dohna and Baron Altenstein from the end of 1808 to the summer of 1810, Hardenberg, who found it easier than Stein to work with the king, had himself appointed state chancellor. In the circumstances, government by prime minister could perhaps best serve the state in its struggle for survival; and possibly the example of Napoleon's Caesarism suggested that one strong individual ought to be placed at the head of the government. That is not to say that Stein abandoned his goal of giving other ministers and senior officials greater scope and of teaching them to cooperate and coordinate their efforts. In his last months in office he moved toward this goal by establishing a so-called general conference of ministers and other high functionaries. The body was short-lived, but under his leadership it legislated extensively and suggests what Stein hoped a true council of state might achieve.

He introduced another fundamental change in the position of the ministers: they no longer administered separate provinces but were now responsible for departments that covered the entire state. Stein had called for this change shortly before the war, in April 1806; delayed by the long French occupation of Prussia, it was finally instituted toward the end of 1808. Departmental ministries were established for interior affairs, finance, foreign affairs, war, and justice. The provincial ministers had represented components of a loosely connected political entity; the new departmental ministers derived from the concept of the unified, centralized state, and their work was guided by a freer, more encompassing point of view.

In creating departmental ministries Stein followed French models. But his method of linking the ministries with the provincial administration revived an older Prussian institution, although in radically different form. This was the office of provincial governor, *Oberpräsident,* an office that Stein himself held in Westphalia until 1804. In the Frederician state the *Oberpräsident* was the chief of a number of war and domain boards; now he became the commissioner or permanent representative of the central ministry in a particular province, charged with coordinating activities of the government in Berlin and the provincial bureaucracy. This office, temporarily introduced during the reform period and definitively established in 1815, had both strong and weak features. As the examples of Vincke in Westphalia and Schön in East Prussia were to show, energetic and creative individuals could become fatherly protectors of their provinces, statesmen who worked both for local concerns and for the state in general.[1] On the other hand, if the holder conceived of his duties in a narrowly bureaucratic rather than political fashion, the position could degenerate into an unnecessary intermediary authority. The office was particularly significant because the provincial governor was made the government's representative in the

1. Ludwig von Vincke (1774–1844) and Theodor von Schön (1773–1856), senior Prussian civil servants, members of the reform party.

reorganized provincial Estates, a role that brought him in close touch with the wishes and interests of the population. As later developments were to show, this experience gave him better insight into social currents than was possessed by the actual administrative authorities in the province, the "governments," into which the old war and domain boards were now transformed.

Stein wanted to open these provincial governments to the new attitudes by giving representatives of the Estates seat and vote on their boards. The representatives' local interests and knowledge of local conditions were to counteract the formalism of the bureaucrats. Stein's "Nassau Memorial" of June 1807 indicates that he saw this infusion as a fundamental reform that would invigorate "community spirit and the spirit of the monarchy." It was an ingenious and impressive conception to oppose the new, more powerful central authorities with a more decentralized organization on the provincial level. The greater the sense of unity at the center, the more readily the people could be granted a share in the administration of their home districts. Under Stein's plan, central and provincial authorities were, so to speak, divided and regrouped differently and more effectively than in Frederician Prussia. Both were to give new opportunities to talent. The emancipation of the heads of the professional bureaucracy, the ministers, and the emancipation of the people from the tutelage of the professional bureaucrat evolved from the same basic idea. But valuable and justified as the idea was, in this instance the method of reform was ill-chosen. Representatives of the Estates and trained officials were too disparate to collaborate successfully in agencies that had developed their own ways of doing things. It meant pouring new wine into old bottles, and the innovation, although tried here and there, was quickly dropped. But the idea of involving private citizens in provincial administration survived, and during the 19th century new vessels appropriate for the new wine were created.

Another significant issue in organizing the new provincial governments was whether Prussia should copy the example of the Napoleonic prefects by giving the head of each "government" dominant authority over his associates, or whether the old collegiate tradition should be continued. The prefectural system was more efficient but also more arbitrary; the collegiate system, in which deliberations and decisions were made as a body, offered greater guarantees for a calm, tolerant handling of affairs, but tended to formalism. In this dilemma between the Scylla of bureaucratic despotism and the Charybdis of bureaucratic pedantry, Stein chose the latter. The new governments, like their predecessors, the war and domain boards, were organized as boards or colleges of councilors. No doubt another reason for Stein's decision was that the representatives of the Estates, whom he wanted to co-opt to the governments, would have been exposed to too much pressure as subordinates of a prefect.

Bureaucratic arbitrariness was further checked by separating judicial and administrative functions. The war and domain boards had had the authority to try most financial and administrative suits; this power was taken from the new governments. Here Stein simply carried out a change that accorded with the spirit of the times, a change demanded by Montesquieu and the Declaration of the Rights of Man, and already introduced in a few Prussian provinces during the attempts at reform before 1806.

According to Stein's conception, the professional bureaucracy was not to reach lower than the provincial governments. Local administration was to be the sphere of self-government and elected officials. This innovation could be based on the existing rural district administration, the *Landkreis,* which was headed by a county councilor, the *Landrat,* who was a representative of—and nominated by—the county Estates, and simultaneously a state official by royal appointment. But in the main the county diet consisted only of noble landowners; towns formed separate districts, headed by a tax councilor, the *Steuerrat.* Stein's promising idea was to combine delegates of the towns and of rural communities with noble landowners in the county diet, which in turn elected the county councilor, who together with a few deputies was to administer the district. Within the districts the towns and rural communities were to administer their own affairs, under the general supervision of the provincial governments. Such a reform would have been difficult to carry out against the resistance of the nobility, which could be expected to defend its former privileges, but Stein's energy would probably have overcome all difficulties. How much his determination meant to the reform program is evident when we see that this particular innovation bogged down as soon as he left office. Stein's immediate successors, Altenstein and Dohna, did little to change local government, but eventually Hardenberg took up the matter and in his *Gendarmerie Edikt* of 30 July 1812 instituted a district constitution that undercut the privileges of the noble landowners but also departed from Stein's ideas of self-government. Under Hardenberg's legislation, each district was to be headed by a director, the *Kreisdirektor,* who was appointed by the state without consulting the local Estates. County deputies, who were to assist him, had only shadowy authority. Hardenberg's edict took too much and gave too little. It replaced the rule of privilege with the rule of bureaucracy and aroused such opposition that the government preferred not to implement it. Hardenberg easily bowed to circumstances; he was sufficiently flexible to relinquish even plans that accorded completely with his concepts of government. During the following decades the authority of the state and the authority of the nobility continued to co-exist in county government, as they had co-existed and supported each other during the *ancien régime.* County government in Stein's spirit of self-administration did not begin until very much later, in 1872.

The Frederician state had treated towns more harshly than the countryside; urban society was regarded as malleable and ineffective. But for that very reason it was now easier to shape and reform urban government. Freedom could be imposed on the towns, just as servitude had once been imposed on them. In consequence Stein's municipal ordinance, the *Städteordnung,* which most fully realized his concept of the state, was issued in the old authoritarian style. Stein did think of consulting representatives of urban groups; but his most important collaborator in this legislation, J. G. Frey, police director of Königsberg, objected that only spokesmen of reactionary, oligarchic, and guild interests would be heard. The immature communities, he argued characteristically, must be led toward maturity, without asking them whether they wanted to go there. Freedom ordained by the lawgiver—that was still enlightened despotism; but it was unavoidable in the absence of political parties or other effective champions of freedom in the population. It was the special mark of Prussia's reforms that a still unpolitical people was to be, and had to be, educated toward political freedom. It was not yet possible to avoid that the state itself act as teacher—the very thing that Wilhelm von Humboldt once abhorred. The intellectual maturity of the men who now legislated had to take the place of the political maturity of the people for whom the laws were decreed. By according the people the duties of freedom, rather than rights that might be excessive and could be abused, by emphasizing political activity rather than political demands, it was possible to overcome the innate difficulty—not to say the internal contradiction—of the whole enterprise of reform.

The French municipal ordinance of 14 December 1789 offered Stein and Frey an instructive model. They agreed with its major aim of breaking the bureaucratic yoke that oppressed the towns, and of transferring the administration of municipal affairs, of the town's property and taxes, to organs elected by the burghers themselves. Since the revolutionary legislation reflected the innate organizational ability of French society and its sense for clear and rational structures, Stein and Frey also borrowed specific articles from the December ordinance. And in general, the radical *élan* that swept through the French model inspired the Prussians with a similar determination not to stop halfway. But they were too solidly grounded in the German past to be swept too far. Because they started with different assumptions they rejected one fundamental concept of the French law. The December ordinance rested on the principle of the political sovereignty of the nation, the French people, from which all other authorities derived and to which they were subordinate. The municipal freedom that the law granted was not given to the towns as distinct political entities but to the part of the nation inhabiting the towns. The town was simply an administrative intermediary between the broad base of the nation and the distillation of the national will, which was expressed in the national assembly and in the executive that derived from it. The town was a section of a pyramid. Consequently, despite its new liberties the town was not free, but dependent on the executive above and on the people below. The elected magistrates had to call a general meeting of voters if a small number of the citizens demanded it. On the other hand, they could not reach certain financial decisions without obtaining approval from the departmental administration. Any corporative spirit that might intervene between state and nation was to be suppressed. Because the whole of France was to become a true republic, no intermediary municipal republics were tolerated; but uniformity endangered the true municipal spirit, which is based on loyalty to the firmly self-sufficient local community.

If the French municipal ordinance was more democratic than republican, Stein's reorganization of city government turned out to be the reverse. It sounds paradoxical, but makes sense after what I have just said, that the still absolutist Hohenzollern monarchy could grant its cities a greater degree of republican autonomy than did the French constitutional monarchy of 1789. The essence and authority of the Prussian kingdom were not endangered by the political independence it offered its cities, which could not compare in number and population with French cities and towns. The basic concept of the new law was drawn from German tradition. Stein and his collaborators consciously reverted to the great age of German cities and to their institutions, those "creations of the public spirit." Stein did not want to abolish the historically rooted intermediary forces between the state, society, and the individual; rather, he wanted to preserve and reshape them. He condemned only their selfish particularism, not their energy. The spontaneous, abundant life of the cities was to enrich and strengthen the whole state.

Consequently he granted the elected members of the new city government an unusual degree of freedom. His faith in self-government made him limit state supervision to a minimum. Government agencies audited the city accounts, resolved complaints of the burghers, and certified new statutes and the election of members of the city council, the magistrates. Nor was the council bound by the will of the community. The deputies, the *Stadtverordneten*, from whom the magistracy was drawn, were elected, but the voters lacked any additional advisory powers. The deputies were to act independently, unaffected by the special interests of the electorate: "The law and the fact of their election constitute their authority, their convictions and their views of the community's general good form their instructions, their conscience is the superior to whom they are responsible." It was hoped that the method of their election would prevent the revival of oligarchic attitudes in the magistrates. Citizens voted for representatives of the districts where they lived, not according to membership in guilds and other corporative bodies. With some exceptions the only disenfranchised inhabitants were those who did not own property in the community, and whose annual income fell below a fixed minimum: 200 taler in cities, 150 taler in medium-sized and small towns. Property-owners were also favored by the regulation that at least two-thirds of the deputies had to own houses and live in the community. We know how much Stein valued the property owner, and can understand why he suppressed a passing impulse to expand the franchise; but he favored propertied residents to such an extent that in years to come their special interests dominated Prussian city government. Stein did not foresee this unhealthy development. He favored the property owner over the unpropertied not for social or economic reasons but on ethical grounds. He believed that men of property would be unchanging in their commitment to the community and more public-spirited than others. Even then that was probably too idealistic a view, and in this instance Stein's romantic ethical ideal clearly hindered future developments and actually achieved the opposite of what he intended. As much as he prized economic activity and supported it by his policies, he always insisted on the ethical conduct of trade and commerce and opposed suppression of the economically weak by the wealthy.

The municipal ordinance established the assembly of elected deputies as the main force in city government. The assembly elected the magistracy composed of city councilors, and in large cities nominated three candidates for the office of mayor. In his dislike of the professional, salaried bureaucrat Stein originally wished to make membership in the magistracy an unsalaried, honorary office, subject to renewal every six years. Eventually he adopted a compromise, by which the mayors were paid but could remain in office only six years. The other councilors were also paid and could hold office for a longer period, but their limited tenure made the councilors dependent on the assembly of deputies. In practice the magistracy became the executive organ of the assembly, carrying out its decisions.

It would have been dubious and risky to separate the process of reaching decisions from that of implementation, with the deputies merely a deliberative parliamentary body. To avoid this danger the deputies themselves were given a share in the management of the public business. "Deputations," made up of deputies and private citizens together with one or two members of the magistracy, were entrusted with much of the city's administration. The deputations supervised schools and churches, the poor houses, hospitals, and other community institutions. These activities gave the concept of unsalaried, voluntary service broad scope for fruitful development.

The freedom French towns had received in the municipal ordinance of 1789 soon declined. The state again overshadowed the urban community, and not until the last decades of the 19th century did municipal autonomy and self-government again become an issue in France. The freedom granted by the Prussian ordinance persisted, despite limitations gradually introduced during the century. This is not to condemn the development in one country or unconditionally praise the course of events in the other. National and political needs were different in France, and even the modern forms of the French concept of the state reflect other standards than the German. But it served Prussia well that toward the end of her absolute phase the state reverted to the German tradition, which emphasized the bonds between the individual and his home and land, his peers and his community, and which granted some autonomy even to the subordinate organs of local government. For the future political freedom in Germany as a whole, Prussia's *Städteordnung* proved an excellent educational tool.

But it should have been complemented by reforms of the rural communities. Similar scope for local administrative and political activity should have been given the peasants. As we know Stein intended to borrow the best features of the Westphalian rural assemblies, and introduce self-government to the Prussian villages. But this was far more difficult to achieve, because in the Central European countryside the institutions and traditions of self-government were much weaker than in the towns. Most rural communities east of the Elbe were small and poor; they were subunits of patrimonial estates or of royal domains, and had developed only a feeble communal life. Their smallness and poverty alone did not pose unsurmountable obstacles to reform, because adjoining settlements might have been combined into aggregate communities or other larger entities. But the position of the squires would have had to be transformed completely. It would have been necessary to abolish or reform their patrimonial jurisdiction, police authority, and patronage. The issue was closely linked with the question of reforming the rural counties, and became entangled in its fate. It was not dropped after Stein's dismissal; interesting plans were drafted, and such statesmanlike individuals as Boyen, who was convinced of the need for introducing political activity to the lower classes as well, never tired of working for it. But the energy and determination for a major political clash with the Prussian nobility had now vanished, and not until 1891 was a law for rural self-government in Stein's spirit enacted, which finally closed this profound gap in the reform program.

To recognize the need for a reform of rural government at the beginning of the century called for political ideals that transcended the issues of the day. The need for reforming agrarian conditions and the relations between landowner and peasant, however, were clearly apparent even then. The war had destroyed the prosperity both of squire and peasant. The government was asked for help, just as people had appealed to it in similar circumstances in earlier years, when the Frederician state could mobilize an entire system of emergency regulations, and tax remissions, that resulted in the benevolent review of individual cases while not affecting basic conditions, a process that involved the entire apparatus of bureaucratic tutelage. Now senior officials shied away from such piecemeal, pedantic welfare, and in any case the state lacked the means to help all deserving cases. Under the pressure of finding comprehensive measures that would not cost the state anything, men naturally turned to modern economic theory, which had long criticized inefficient traditional agrarian practices and predicted new prosperity for landowner and peasant once the old restrictions were lifted. But the economic emancipation of the peasant was also regarded as his moral emancipation. As the edict of 9 October 1807 declared, it was "commensurate with the essential demands of justice as well as with the principles of well-regulated economic activity to abolish everything that until now has prevented the individual from attaining that measure of prosperity that it is within his power to attain." What before 1806 had been done for the peasants on the royal domains was now extended to the "private" peasants on the manorial estates. Another political reason for proceeding without delay was the liberation of the peasants announced in the new constitution of the Grand-Duchy of Warsaw, created from the Polish provinces lost by Prussia at the Peace of Tilsit. Finally, in East Prussia this reform simply meant accelerating a process already under way, because many East Prussian landowners were replacing their peasants' obligatory duties with paid labor.

When Stein arrived in East Prussia early in October 1807 he found waiting for him drafts of the edict that was to proclaim him as a liberator throughout the world. The drafts were primarily the work of East Prussian bureaucrats, among whom Theodor von Schön in particular was a radical champion of the gospel of Adam Smith and Jakob Kraus and of other reformist concepts that had long been popular in East Prussia. But the edict's most significant clauses merely repeated what Stein had suggested years earlier in Westphalia. It was as though the eastern and western spheres of progressive thought in Prussia joined to reform the entire state. At Stein's arrival it was still uncertain whether the edict should initially apply to East and West Prussia alone, or whether it should be introduced everywhere. The king had desired the more comprehensive step, but was dissuaded by two cautious senior officials, the brothers Friedrich Leopold and Karl Wilhelm von Schrötter. Stein's firmness gave the king new resolve. The two men met halfway in the decision to apply the new benefits of the edict to the whole state at once.

The edict did more than emancipate the peasant. It also offered the landowner compensation for the loss he had suffered in the war and would suffer by the emancipation. This intention to compensate the landowning nobility distinguished Prussia's agrarian reforms from the French agrarian revolution of 4 August 1789. However we may feel about this difference, it would never have been possible to impose reforms against the opposition of the landowners. They still constituted the wealthiest and most powerful group in society, and Prussia lacked a socially and economically strong middle class that might have helped the state to defeat the nobles. The true opponent of the nobility was the higher bureaucracy, which had begun to incorporate the interests of the aspiring third Estate but did not represent these interests forcefully and directly. Instead it gave them a different psychological and political cast, and in a sense made them more abstract. The social dominance of the nobility was attacked less by other social elements than by the ideals of the reformers, and these ideals called not for destruction of the nobility but for its improvement. Many reformers were themselves noblemen; they felt themselves to be innovators and teachers, not renegades. That is particularly true of Stein, and for that reason he could accept those clauses of the edict that favored the landowner as readily as he accepted those that did not.

The nobility lost almost at one stroke all benefits it had derived from the peasants' hereditary servitude—*Erbuntertänigkeit*: "After St. Martin's day of 1810 hereditary servitude is abolished in all of our territories. After St. Martin's day all our people are free." The edict did not list the duties contained in the term *Erbuntertänig-keit*—a little vague and sloppy in this, as was much of the reform legislation. But clearly the peasant no longer had to obtain his lord's permission to move from the estate, or to marry, or to have his children learn a trade, or send them to school. His children were no longer obliged to perform domestic service on the estate. Henceforth the peasant owed his lord only those obligations that a free man "derived from the tenure of land or from a special contract."

The free economy proclaimed by the edict was to benefit both the nobility and the peasants. We recall that the structure of society into three Estates had become so ingrained that categories of noble and non-noble land had developed, which could not be sold freely on the open market. These barriers fell. Any nobleman could now acquire peasant or burgher land, and peasants and burghers could buy noble manors without special permission. Enlarging the number of prospective buyers and easing the transfer of ownership was also intended to raise land values. But the edict went beyond agrarian matters to remove the restrictions that limited particular occupations to particular Estates. It decreed that "every nobleman is free to take up middle-class occupations without loss of status; every peasant is free to become a burgher, and every burgher to become a peasant." At least in the eyes of the legislators and the law the nature of "Estate" itself was changed by breaking the legal bond that had linked each individual to a particular social group. Estates turned into classes, which men could enter as they wished and according to the extent of their economic resources. It is true that burghers and peasants couldn't simply become noblemen, but they were free to take up noble occupations and assume the manner of life of the nobility. It was hoped that social conditions would evolve similar to those in England, where the gentry was made up of noble and non-noble landowners, and the younger sons of the nobility entered middle-class life and could work their way up again through commerce and trade.

But legislation alone could not destroy the roots of the old system and create a new society. Attitudes had to change as well. Traditional views were still too strongly held for the average Prussian Junker to benefit from his new occupational freedom. To a far greater extent than the reformers wished, the nobility retained the character of an Estate. In the course of the 19th century, bourgeoisie and peasantry gradually changed into true classes with fluctuating boundaries, but the nobility stubbornly retained its old forms and clung to the view that apart from working one's land only government service or the army provided occupations appropriate to a nobleman. Only a few nobles entered other classes; conversely the many newcomers to the nobility further increased its size and significance. Usually the burgher who bought a manorial estate, and the bourgeois officer or official who was ennobled, adopted the Junker's style of life within two or three generations at the latest. The nobility did not always accept these newcomers as equals, but it was happy to use their energies to further strengthen its influence and power.

The ultimate effects of the edict of October 1807 thus differed considerably from the intent of the law and from Stein's wishes. The petty nobility was not diminished but rather rejuvenated and increased, and, while abolishing class and occupational restrictions did help some individuals, the edict also fortified the class spirit of the Junkers. A similarity exists in the ways in which the nobility and the Catholic Church have responded to modern freedom. Emancipation and reform actually brought great advantages to any group with significant economic resources, since it could exploit the greater mobility that resulted from the destruction of old barriers. Although the church and the nobility were deprived of privileges and institutions that once had helped them grow to power, they were now strong enough to do without them and to compete effectively in the new condition of freedom. The Catholic Church in Germany lost her territorial possessions and her autonomous ecclesiastical principalities, the nobility lost its economic privileges and the hereditary servitude of its peasants—what did that matter if the new freedom brought new advantages!

In fact the Prussian nobility quickly recognized the possible benefits of the agrarian reforms. No-one could yet predict the increase in the size of the nobility that would occur in the course of the 19th century, an increase that the nobility as a group did very little to encourage, but the Junkers could and did count on increasing their holdings if they were now free to remove tenants or buy up peasant land. Until the October edict the state had systematically protected peasant land against incorporation in manorial estates.

Now the Junkers regarded the right to enlarge their estates by purchasing peasant land as natural compensation for losing the rights of hereditary servitude. The right they claimed was the right of the economically stronger over the economically weaker.

Stein opposed their claim. We have said that he did not want unlimited economic freedom, but an economy guided by ethical and social values. "Only *one* legal limitation on the free disposition of property must be retained," he wrote at the time, "the limitation that restricts the self-interest of the wealthy and educated, and prevents absorption of peasant land into their estates." But the conditions of the time did not permit rigorous observance of this principle, in which for once Stein's views were in accord with the social policies of the Frederician state. The war had so severely hurt many farming villages in East and West Prussia that agricultural productivity could be reestablished only by transferring part of the village holdings for better or worse to the landowner. Consequently the October edict authorized local administrations to approve the amalgamation of farms that were no longer productive into larger holdings, or their incorporation into manorial estates.

The landowners eagerly grasped everything offered them by the edict and by its still more generous executive regulations. An observer commented in 1812 that their universal compulsion for enlarging their holdings was enormously stimulated. Had they owned more capital, "the larger estates would by now have swelled into unwieldy masses, and have swallowed up the respectable and useful class of small-holders."

Had Stein remained in office he probably would have been strong enough to put some brakes on this process. His successors, who continued the agrarian reforms, lacked his power. The new economic theory of *laissez faire* coincided with the expansionist bent of the landowners; between them peasant and peasant land were ground as between two millstones. The friction became even greater when under Hardenberg the government turned to the issue of peasant land that in one form or another was already part of a noble estate.

Landholding rights and service obligations of the peasantry differed greatly in degree and kind. A few peasants were completely independent, but their number was relatively significant only in East and West Prussia, where some peasants had lived as free

"Kölmer" since the days of the Teutonic Order, under the charter drawn up at that time in the city of Kulm. Most peasants lived on noble estates, and fell into three main categories: (1) peasants who were hereditary leaseholders, *Erbpächter*; (2) peasants who had the usufruct of the land, either in hereditary or nonhereditary tenure, *Lassiten*; (3) peasants holding temporary leases, *Zeitpächter*. All three groups, but especially the second, owed the lord not only dues in money and kind, but also the manual and team labor that worked the estate. The guiding idea of the agrarian reforms was to remove these duties, which were now considered to be both uneconomical and degrading, and turn tenure into true ownership. But this goal was only partly realized. The edict of 14 September 1811 on peasants holding hereditary or nonhereditary tenure and peasants holding temporary leases, ruled that the former should cede one-third of the land he occupied, whereas the temporary leaseholder should turn over half his land to the lord. This compensation was highly advantageous to the landlord. The peasant became an independent landowner, but his acreage was truncated while the manorial estate increased considerably in size. The landlord now faced the problem of finding labor for his enlarged holdings, and the Junkers demanded that the new regulations should exclude certain categories of peasant land, whose occupants were to provide compulsory service as before. Again Hardenberg accommodated the nobility by issuing an amendment to the edict, the so-called declaration of 29 May 1816, a law of major economic as well as social and political impact. Under the amendment those peasants were excluded from the edict of 1811—did not qualify for regulation, as the phrase went—who did not own a team of draft animals, as well as those whose farms were not registered in the official tax records, or whose tenure was of relatively recent origin. At the same time the last barriers against buying up peasant land disappeared. The landlord was now permitted to purchase the entire holdings of a tenant farmer or temporary leaseholder, if the peasant agreed to sell and had not yet ceded his share under the edict of 1811. But the landlord could also exploit the loophole in the law to buy out those peasants who did not qualify for regulation. In short he could do what he wanted, depending on whether he was more interested in obtaining cheap labor or additional land. After the war, when labor became less scarce, most of the peasants excluded from regulation were in fact reduced to the condition of day-laborers or at best became temporary tenant farmers.

Only if we regard the landed nobility as the mainstay of the Prussian people can this development, and the social conditions and power relationships it caused in the course of the century, be considered salutary. But we can regret this development and yet think it unavoidable. It is possible to argue that at the time the beleaguered state had no choice but to offer very generous compensation to that group in society on whose political support it depended. On the other hand, the state's internal authority was not all that weak, nor—to its credit—was the landed nobility so selfish that only significant rewards could induce it to sacrifice for the state and nation. No doubt the agrarian policies of Hardenberg's ministry were convenient, but there was no compelling need for them.

And yet, despite their social flaws Hardenberg's policies did create scope for the economic development urgently needed by the state and the people as a whole. More rational and intensive working of the land now became possible. The replacement of compulsory labor with paid labor, the separation of manorial estate and peasant land, the simultaneous partition of common land—these changes made the individual farmer more dependent on his own resources and encouraged innovation. The corporative spirit of agriculture gave way to individual enterprise. On the other hand, the meager protection that the state once gave to small and unproductive holdings now fell away. During the next decades many families lost their land and emigrated to the cities, where they soon became victims of the new urban economy that the reform legislation had helped create. The displaced peasantry formed a major source for the armies of workers that were required by the industrialization and capitalism of the 19th century.

The abolition of guild monopolies and the removal of all occupational barriers, which Stein prepared, were promulgated by Hardenberg's edicts of 2 November 1810 and 7 September 1811. Like the municipal ordinance this achievement belonged to the reformers alone, a benefit that the people had not demanded but which the government granted. In a sense it was the final accomplishment of the enlightened absolutism that for so long had controlled the economy, and which with new insight now removed the barriers that held back enterprise, individual competition, and stilled the flow of capital. But although the benefits of the municipal ordinance were recognized at once, those of the new occupational freedom were not. The urban groups whom it was to benefit regarded it as a disaster and heatedly opposed it. Their position is understandable if we recall that the guild system and the absence of occupational barriers represented two fundamentally opposed attitudes, and that the traditional point of view was too ingrained by the habit of centuries to be eradicated by legislative fiat. Guilds were based on the belief that the livelihood of the individual artisan or tradesman must be assured and, equally, that the consumer must be protected by control of the quality and price of goods. The system was a compromise between producers and consumers and among the guild members themselves; it aimed at maintaining standards rather than at the aggressive increase of wealth. Within this controlled economy men could feel protected and comfortable without recognizing the debilitating effects that were apparent to the outside observer. Consequently the government's sudden intervention, which abruptly threw the artisan into the competitive arena, was experienced as a brutal attack, and even—with some justification—as an assault on ethical values. Men complained that uncontrolled competition led to greed, dishonesty, and shoddy workmanship, and that it under-mined integrity and discipline, all of which contrasted unfavorably with the corporative spirit and patriarchal institutions of the guilds. In themselves these traditional elements had some merit, but they were too closely linked to the quietude and smugness of the past to be preserved. Significant reforms are always painful; every advance in political or social life has its price. The ideal that the new freedom of occupation imposed, so to speak, on the commercial bourgeoisie may be called the mobilization of all energies in the struggle for economic existence. Certainly that ideal incorporates selfish motives, but were these absent in the old ways?

Modern ethics, as they evolved from the social and economic upheavals of the 19th century, do not regard it as ignoble for man to struggle, and to create goods beyond his immediate needs. Those who falter in this struggle should not be overlooked, but neither should we deny the moral power of creative work. The new industrial Germany emerged from these efforts—a clear illustration of the interaction between the reformers' humanistic ideals and the realistic attitudes and creativity of the following period.

[87

But again we may ask whether the reformers' bold, optimistic break with tradition was not too abrupt. Had Stein remained in office he would no doubt have proceeded more cautiously. Later he even felt some longing for bygone patriarchal values, and regretted the hasty destruction of the guilds. One condition, however, no-one could want to bring back after it had been eradicated by the new occupational freedom: the separation of town and countryside, which had kept the rural population dependent on the urban economy. By permitting villagers to become artisans and engage in trade the government destroyed the old system of taxation with its dualism of excise and land tax. Hardenberg's uncertain experimentation could not immediately discover a suitable replacement, but Stein pointed to the future when he temporarily levied an income tax on the English model in East and West Prussia.

Not only was the East Prussian income tax of 1808 a promising concept, it came into being according to the constitutional principle of no taxation without representation. The tax was debated and approved by a convention of the East Prussian Estates, which Stein transformed from a pure organ of the nobility into a provisional assembly representing all groups. But he did not intend to stop with provincial assemblies that took a hand in local administration. A national assembly was to crown the reforms, a Prussian parliament that would close the last gap between state and nation. "For the nation to share in legislation and administration," he said, "creates a love of the constitution, an informed public opinion in national affairs, and in many individual citizens the capacity for administering the public business." This, his ultimate reform, like the other elements of the reform program, was not meant to give the nation—the people—a political weapon against the government, but had the ethical intent of developing the nation's attitudes and capabilities, and of forming individuals who would serve all society according to the principle: "History teaches us that many more great commanders and statesmen have emerged under free constitutions than in despotic states."

Since Stein always accepted a hierarchic society as the natural link between individual and nation, he rejected the Revolutionary concept of a national assembly elected by the entire people. The projected Prussian assembly was to be based on Estates and occupational groupings; all property owners had the right to vote. Stein's deepest concern was to prevent the nobility from dominating the assembly, and it is significant that he weighed a fairly extensive reform of the nobility in connection with the constitutional projects of the fall of 1808. After his previous experiences he regarded the Prussian nobles as a burden on the nation: there were too many of them, most of them poor, and consequently they were both under-educated and too demanding. Stein wanted to reduce the nobility to a small number of wealthy families, which could develop into a politically sophisticated aristocracy to serve the nation. Together with distinguished men of all classes they would form the upper house of the future parliament. Since the nation was still politically inexperienced, Stein intended to give this body only modest powers at first: the right to debate legislation, but also the authority to initiate laws.

The project reveals Stein's practicality, but also his ideals, which rose far above the practical world. Realistic elements and fantasy coexisted in his thought, but the impractical aspects of his scheme of a national parliament would probably have disappeared in the course of electing and organizing such a body, which by the fall of 1808 had become a major goal for the entire reform party. On 29 September Boyen warmly recommended the project to the king: on 14 October Scharnhorst, Gneisenau, Schön, and other friends urged Stein to proceed; and three weeks later the king went so far as to approve a draft by the convocation of East Prussian Estates, which already discussed the future nationwide organization of the Estates. A change of this magnitude, however, would have dwarfed all other reforms, and was linked more directly than these to the great issue of the state's survival. Stein and his allies valued a national parliament not only for its own sake, but also saw it as a weapon in the war of liberation that they were considering at the time, and as one of the stimuli that Stein thought necessary to rouse the peaceful German burgher. The political rights that parliamentary representation was to give the nation were now to serve, above all, to awaken enthusiasm for the coming war. Had a parliament been instituted at that time it would have proved a heroic beginning for Prussian constitutional life.

But by regarding parliament as a weapon in the fight against Napoleon, Stein intertwined the project with his policy of national liberation and with his own fate. His fall from power meant the end of the scheme, and his successors Altenstein and Dohna did not revive it. Hardenberg again took it more seriously. In his view a national parliament was essential to complete the reorganization of the state; but he thought of it less as a vigorous political organ of the nation than as a governmental organ, which might prove useful if carefully organized and treated with the necessary caution. Unlike Stein he was not guided by the ideal of unity of state and nation; instead he approached the essentially unbureaucratic institution of popular representation in a highly bureaucratic spirit. "The new representative assembly," he declared, "must be the work of the government alone, it must come from above like a charitable gift," and "great care must be taken to ensure that no obstructive resistance to government measures will be organized, which would lead to general ruin." In February 1811 he experimented by calling a national assembly of notables to debate the new tax system. Gneisenau condemned the move as a mere "government device" to make the financial burdens somewhat more appealing. While the notables were meeting, the Brandenburg nobility, which also favored a national assembly of Estates, but one that it could dominate, protested so strongly against Hardenberg's policies that the chancellor felt the need to retaliate. In the summer of 1811 the opposition leaders, the obstinate, gifted August von der Marwitz, and Count Finckenstein,[2] who in a memorial had dared to appeal to the rights of the *old* Estates, and alluded to Hardenberg's poor administration, were locked up in the citadel of Spandau for a few weeks. But the conflict was little more than sham. It irritated Hardenberg that the nobility disturbed his bureaucratic designs, but he was prepared to let the nobility play a dominant role within the firm bureaucratic structure of government. We recall to what an extent his agrarian legislation of 1811 favored the nobility, and the Junkers were over-represented in the assembly of notables. The successor of this body, a provisional national assembly that met from 1812 to 1815, was elected by both county and city councils, but the 18 noble deputies were joined by only 12 deputies of the cities and 9 deputies of the

2. August Ludwig von der Marwitz (1777–1837), Prussian soldier. His essays and memoirs constitute the most forceful literary expression of aristocratic conservatism in Prussia. Friedrich Ludwig Finck von Finckenstein (1745–1818), president of the "government" of the Mark Brandenburg, and a leader of the conservative nobility.

peasantry. The assembly achieved little, but what it did favored the landed nobility. It was the body that drafted the declaration of 29 May 1816, which gave the agrarian reforms such an ominous turn. That Hardenberg would not let the assembly become more than advisory is understandable, but even in that form he did not know how to work with it or foster the political energies that occasionally stirred in its debates. The assembly's ineffectual existence certainly did not prove that national representation in general was impossible or useless. Whoever wanted to create a true parliament would have to begin by politically educating the public, as Stein had hoped to do; but unlike Hardenberg such a teacher would have had to believe honestly in political freedom.

But under the best circumstances it might have been unrealistic to try to teach freedom to a people that lacked all political experience and that, except for its aristocratic elite, had never evinced real desire for political action. Political experience, which could come about only through self-government, needed time to develop. Can one compare the political wishes now occasionally expressed in bourgeois circles with, for example, the political excitement of the French in 1789? Nevertheless, two factors seem to justify the constitutional plans held by Stein and his associates. The first are the moral and patriotic sentiments that now began to move the lower classes, not only educated men. The disasters of 1806 and of the following years made the nation conscious of its bonds to the dynasty and the state. The king's simple dignity and the queen's nobility in the face of humiliation awakened emotions in burgher and peasant, which their own suffering at the hands of the French could intensify to silent hatred. Constitutional life could not have begun more auspiciously than with an assembly of true representatives of the people, called by the king on the eve of the wars of liberation. Weighing all factors carefully, Humboldt wrote in 1810 that "in general the nation is good, and . . . is ready for every deprivation and every sacrifice."

Secondly, while the lower classes substituted loyalty for their lack of political experience, the educated bourgeoisie could point to its intellectual and cultural achievements to justify its hopes for new political rights. No one raised violent demands for a constitution; but, more important and more promising, men genuinely wished to serve the state and the fatherland with their intellectual powers.

Not that the arts and sciences were to serve political ends directly, and change their character for this purpose. That was the policy of the Napoleonic Empire, which no one wanted to follow. One day, Altenstein said, artists and scientists would revenge themselves on Napoleon by pursuing the superior tendency of truth, and ensuring its victory. That conviction was shared by Wilhelm von Humboldt, whose position in the Ministry of the Interior now made him the principal intermediary between government and culture. The sacrifices of the impoverished state for the arts and sciences would, he hoped, strongly influence the mind and character of the Prussian people, but it should not be an influence that could be forced and shaped: "The state's true, permanent interest consists in the free development of the nation's cultural energies." This freedom was given to the new University of Berlin, which in 1810 was founded according to Humboldt's plans. The great teachers with which the university began—men like Fichte, Schleiermacher, Niebuhr, and Savigny—showed that it had become possible to be both an independent scholar and a passionate patriot. At this same time Prussia's greatest poet, Heinrich von Kleist, sought to offer his dramatic genius to the service of state and nation. Hardenberg's petty rejection of the poet, whose entreaties were becoming a nuisance to him, contributed to Kleist's suicide in the fall of 1811. The event shows that the alliance between the autonomous mind and the state was far from harmonious. But in general both sides believed in the need for the alliance and felt that it must be free from constraints.

In a sense this alliance also abolished the old belief in the limited functions of government. Men began to feel that service to the community was a cause as unlimited and infinite as art and philosophy, and the development of one's own individuality. Some intellectuals who served the state as bureaucrats or officers were no longer content with their limited duties. Men and conditions being what they were, the new attitude could hardly coalesce into a genuine political movement. But a multitude of patriotic activities came into being, all moving toward one goal, and some seeking to unite into a larger force. The particular group or activity might appear narrow and impractical, but the urge for free and effective action was evident. Artificiality and constraints but also aspirations existed side by side in many people, and are exemplified by the famous "Association of Virtue," or, as it called itself, the "Moral-scientific

Society," which a group of officials, officers, and scholars founded in Königsberg in April 1808. The society's statutes could not declare that its ultimate purpose was to prepare for the coming war of liberation. Some of the leading reformers, among whom Boyen and Grolman became members, supported the society, without overestimating the effectiveness of its partly innocuous, partly absurd methods. It disbanded after less than two years, without achieving anything more than a strengthening of the patriotic and idealistic convictions that had given it birth. Had war broken out at the time, the society would presumably have played a more active role. Stein had such expectations, and some of the society's members were in fact beginning to organize cells in the provinces.

The awkwardness these men showed when they attempted to act as citizens and engage in politics contrasted with the determination and confidence with which the actual reformers carried out their task. The reformers had the advantage of being able to employ traditions and methods of the absolutist state to achieve innovation. At the same time they showed the secret and open enemies of reform at court and in the army, who believed only in tradition and routine, that the maximum of state power could not be achieved unless the Frederician tradition merged with the new humanistic and national spirit. By creating such a union in the army the reformers gave the crippled state an instrument of power it did not have before.

If we wish to summarize Prussia's military reforms, we can say that the army was transformed from a mere tool in the hands of the commander-in-chief into a living institution. The army was not taken out of the monarch's control; but from now on it carried out his orders in a different, more independent manner. The ancient bond linking army and ruler was strengthened by new spiritual ties that encouraged spontaneity and individuality.

A transformation of this magnitude would have been impossible in Prussia without the king's express consent. In the so-called Ortelsburg Publicandum of 1 December 1806 and in later memoranda, Frederick William outlined ideas for reform that coincided with Scharnhorst's views, but which Scharnhorst and Gneisenau expanded and radicalized. Immediately after the Peace of Tilsit Scharnhorst was promoted to major-general and made head of the Military Reorganization Commission, to which the king appointed Gneisenau but also other, less suitable and less progressive men.

Gradually Scharnhorst managed to replace the most obstructionist members with his own friends and supporters, Boyen, who was devoted to him, and Grolman and Goetzen, both exceptionally bold and energetic soldiers.[3]

Like Stein, Scharnhorst soon came into conflict with the king's cabinet, which raised obstacles to changing the army. This conflict ended differently from the way it had in the civilian realm. The military cabinet, the so-called General Adjutant's Office, was not abolished because the close personal relationship between the Hohenzollern monarchs and their soldiers demanded that the king, through his cabinet, could intervene in the army's affairs. But the men who held the position of general adjutant were changed. Until now the general adjutant might be almost any infantry officer; no special expertise was required. Possibly through Stein's intervention, Scharnhorst succeeded in June 1808 in having himself appointed in place of the unsuitable holder of the position. The following year the General Adjutant's Office was incorporated into the new central military agency, the Ministry of War, which was created on 1 March 1809 as one of the five new ministries of state. The Ministry of War was organized into two principal departments: the General War Department, and the Economic Department. The former was divided into three sections, the first of which carried out the main functions of the old general adjutant's office. Under the supervision of the director of the General War Department, the head of the first section reported to the king on personnel matters. Since the king tended to trust a few confidential advisers, the head of the first section might acquire influence in his own right. But in the years of reform, when the position was usually occupied by such friends of Scharnhorst as Boyen and Grolman, it was easy to reconcile the functions of a responsible minister of war with the monarch's personal intervention.

One goal Scharnhorst never achieved: he was not officially appointed minister of war. For the time being the position remained open. But as director of the General War Department he was the effective head of the ministry. His subordinates were young and energetic men, the best among the military reformers, determined,

3. Karl Wilhelm von Grolman (1777-1843) and Friedrich Wilhelm von Goetzen (1767-1820), leading military reformers.

in Scharnhorst's words, "to lift and invigorate the army's spirit; to bring army and nation more closely together; and to guide the army toward its great task." With such statements Scharnhorst tried to counter the opposition of men who criticized details of innovation while failing to comprehend the purpose of the whole. We will see that the parts as well as the whole were well thought out and proved effective.

Let us summarize the achievements of the years from 1807 to 1812, and turn first to the reorganization of the army, carried out in 1807 and 1808. Even this first phase of the military reforms was based on principles that were to permeate the new force. Officers who had betrayed their trust during the fighting, or otherwise shared responsibility for the defeats of 1806, were brought to trial. The disgraceful capitulations of whole armies and of major fortresses were investigated, and all units that had surrendered were disbanded forever, even though many had long and distinguished records. Of the infantry regiments in the new army, only seven could trace their history to the period before 1806.

The reformers planned to raise a large number of cadres, which could be quickly expanded into combat formations. But they were handicapped by the Convention of 8 September 1808, in which France fixed the rate of reparations and restricted Prussia's armed strength. The Convention not only limited the army's peacetime strength to 42,000 men; it also limited the number of regiments, a provision that was particularly obstructive to future expansion. The Prussian government nevertheless risked greatly exceeding the permitted number of cavalry units, so that by 1809 the army was made up of 19 regiments of cavalry, 12 of infantry, and 3 elite light infantry battalions. Scharnhorst was especially concerned with strengthening the artillery, the branch of the service in which he had spent his early years. Most of its equipment had been lost or destroyed in the war. Now he set up a broad rearmament program to produce new, improved weapons. Even more important, by increasing the batteries' peacetime allotment of draft horses he made realistic field training possible.

The reorganization of the various branches of the army raised their efficiency and flexibility. At the same time their interaction was improved by a division of the entire force into six brigades, each made up of infantry, cavalry, and artillery. The army became a group of small, self-sufficient entities. The mechanical standardization of the old line of battle was replaced by permanently integrated commands, in which the same regiments and batteries served in peacetime and in war.

Scharnhorst was less interested in drill and polish than in realistically preparing the troops for war. He mobilized all available moral and physical resources to gain combat efficiency. Drill fields became places very different from what they had been before 1806. In those days target practice for the rank and file was practically unheard-of since the entire tactical system was based on massive, unaimed volleys. Now the new instruction on the training of troops of 3 June 1808 emphasized the importance of target practice. Skirmishing, the significant tactical innovation of the French, depended on the aimed fire of the individual soldier, and skirmishing was now adopted by the Prussian line. Small field exercises were organized for the infantry and cavalry to accustom them to work together. Formal guard duties and other ceremonies that took up excessive time and energy before 1806 were sharply reduced. Officers were no longer assigned their own pack horses, and elegant infantry lieutenants had to descend from their personal mounts and from now on march with the troops and carry their own knapsacks. The soldiers lost their large squad tents and were issued overcoats instead. Since the baggage and supply trains were greatly reduced, the troops were authorized, and indeed ordered, to requisition in enemy territory.

A breath of fresh air swept through the traditional service routine. The old ballast fell away, not to make soldiers more comfortable but to make them better fighters. But we must remember that this ballast had accumulated over generations and once had even been necessary in order to balance the army's effectiveness with its social characteristics. Tradition could not simply be decreed out of existence without being replaced by counterweights, which in their own way would secure the army's moral and psychological cohesiveness.

The triumphant new generation of ambitious French leaders made it evident that the Prussian officer corps needed to be revitalized. Its aristocratic exclusivity had to be broken down, the practice of automatic promotion according to seniority to be reformed, and scope given to talent and to justified ambition. In short, individual and personal as well as general patriotic motives had to be reinforced in the officer corps.

Strangely radical proposals to bring this about were put forward by two civilians, Hardenberg and Altenstein. In the spirit of the French Revolution they called for election of noncommissioned officers by the rank and file, and election of junior officers by the NCO's. This innovation would have run counter to the whole trend of modern military institutions, which separated officers and rank and file, and gave officers absolute authority. The reformers chose a different way to channel new talent to the army. Once again they found a general standard in their own personal ideals. They regarded themselves an elite of talents, intellectually and profession-ally ambitious, but an elite rooted in the nation as a whole. The entire officer corps was to be reformed in this image. The preferen-tial treatment of the nobleman was to end. The officer's authority over his men remained absolute, but it was now to be justified by his intellectual and moral superiority. The imperfect but unavoid-able method for choosing this elite was to be a system of examin-ations. According to the regulation of 6 August 1808, candidates for commissions no longer entered the army as officer-cadets but as privates. They had to demonstrate a minimum level of academic competence before they were appointed to the rank of ensign, and pass a second examination for promotion to lieutenant. Noncom-missioned officers were not excluded from commissions if they could pass the officer's examination. To give due weight not only to the candidate's knowledge but also to his character and personality, officers already serving in his regiment were empowered to nominate candidates and to confirm their promotion. This was to stimulate, as well, a healthy corporative spirit in the regiment, while the closed guild-mentality was countered by the practice of no longer appointing the regimental commander according to strict seniority, but by choosing him from all field-grade officers regardless of length of service. The corporative spirit linked with an emphasis on individual qualities also provided the basis for new disciplinary regulations. Penalties were made to accord with the more refined and humane concepts of honor of the age, while courts of honor were established in each regiment to safeguard the moral standards of its officers, and reduce the incidence of official punishment.

The system of company economy, which had subjected the

company commander to severe temptations by turning him into an entrepeneur, was abolished in 1807 and 1808. From now on the company's books were audited; any funds saved on equipment, uniforms, and food were returned to the state. At the same time, fixed pay scales were introduced, and supplemental combat pay was promised in wartime.

Military education was more simply and rationally organized. The three institutes for advanced study that existed before 1806— the academies for artillery and engineering, and Scharnhorst's academy for young officers—were combined into a single school for officers in Berlin. Besides training gunners and engineers, the new school also prepared officers from all branches for the General Staff and for service as adjutants to senior commanders. Below this apex, three military schools prepared ensigns for their second examination. On the lowest level were the cadet schools. Since they had essentially been institutions for the nobility the reformers wanted to abolish them, but the king refused to go that far. At least the cadet schools were now to give preferential admission to sons of officers killed in action, whether or not they were nobles.

But all in all, the officer corps was not radically changed. It was given institutions that derived from the rational, systematic spirit of modern administration and from the national and individualistic spirit of the educated classes; but the tradition of the officer corps as a corporation held together by unique attitudes and qualities was not abandoned. To be sure, the reformers attempted to change these attitudes, with some success. But just because the officer corps was a corporation and was to remain one, it had to be given some latitude for further development. In the course of time this development carried the officer corps back to its aristocratic, old-Prussian roots, and former qualities reasserted themselves more than the reformers had wished. Nevertheless the officer corps was revitalized, and its new vigor was due not only to its innate energy but also to the innovations that had been introduced.

Reforming the officer corps meant grafting new elements on an existing, independent organism. Reforming the rank and file first meant bringing to life an inert, passive mass. The Frederician soldier had been a means to an end, little more than a machine. Now the ideal of German neo-humanism, man as an end in himself, had to be realized for the common soldier. It was a demand of the age as well as of the reformers, who had held that ideal since their youth. With particular force and clarity the treatment of the soldier revealed the lesson that Fichte had learned during his own development: in the present age universal human values must seek their realization in the framework of the nation. But human dignity could not simply be assigned to the soldier, as the Enlightenment had sometimes imagined. The soldier's road to dignity led through the nation. If he could regard the harsh duties of his calling not solely as external restraints but also as innate personal obligations toward the fatherland, then he changed into the moral individual idealized by neo-humanism. And the humanistic ideal itself ascended another step by entering a broader reality, by illuminating not only the small elite of creative minds but by bringing light and life to all. Only with this step did neo-humanism finally reach its full potential.

The ideals of humanism and patriotism had always foundered on the army's historically and politically conditioned structure, particularly on the many foreigners serving in the ranks. The changed political situation actually favored the ideals. The Peace of Tilsit threw the Prussian state entirely on its own resources and closed off any foreign territory where it might have recruited soldiers in significant numbers. To regain military strength nothing remained but to accept the new conditions, renounce foreign recruitment and mobilize one's native resources more intensively.

A statesman of the *ancien régime* would have done just that in similar situations. But the reformers recognized that they could raise the army's effectiveness still further if they mobilized not only bodies but also convictions. Flights of idealistic policy had to be risked if new concrete power was the goal. Scharnhorst and his associates were at once realistic politicians and idealists when they demanded universal conscription. They demanded more than realistic calculations called for, because continuing to exempt the educated and propertied classes would have meant losing only a small number of conscripts. How small was the upper stratum at that time, how much could the manpower pool have been expanded if only the former exemptions of the urban population, which spared the tradesmen and small property owners, had been eliminated! The reformers demanded even more than the supreme realist of the age, Napoleon, thought necessary to demand from the French nation. Conscription, that significant achievement of the Revolution, remained law in the Empire, but Napoleon permitted the sons of the wealthy to buy themselves off by providing a substitute. In this way he secured for himself the enormous manpower of the nation while placing the bourgeoisie in his debt. Even reform-minded Prussian officials thought this compromise politically realistic, and sufficient to meet the army's needs at least in peacetime. Scharnhorst's circle, however, thought it not only cheapened the dignity of the nation but believed it to be dangerously divisive. Napoleon may have correctly read the concerns of the French people of his day when he offered them a compromise between the ideas of 1789 and the egotism of the propertied classes. But Scharnhorst, Boyen, and Gneisenau equally understood their Germans when they declared, in Scharnhorst's words: "In implementing a universal principle, the principle must be preserved in all its noble purity if we wish to affect the mind of the citizen." It was characteristic of German intellectuals that they defended their ideals mercilessly against external additions, and subordinated matter to spirit. Perhaps Germans in general were, at that time, more sensitive than Frenchmen to any falsification or clouding of the ideals held out to them. If they were now called upon to form a national army, this army had to be a genuinely national force. This seemed to follow from Kant's categorical imperative and perhaps also from the still intense religiosity of the German people. A report of the conscription commission to the king on 1 July 1809 argued that "if the peasant and poor burgher sees that he is forced to take up arms while members of another class are exempt from this duty, then he cannot regard war for king and fatherland as a holy necessity that supercedes everything else." Implementing the principle in all its purity also meant raising its effects to the utmost. According to the reformers' highly realistic conception, the youth of the educated classes were to act as yeast for the army as a whole, and give it the moral and intellectual superiority that so far had not accompanied the raw courage of the armies fighting against France.

For the time being the reformers did not succeed with their demands. But they took some essential preparatory steps, and, once the external political situation changed, their plans were far enough advanced for conscription to be introduced at once. First it was necessary to reform the treatment and discipline of the rank and file, so that, in Gneisenau's words, the soldier was no longer motivated by the stick beating on his back but by a sense of honor. The Prussian army was given this "liberty of the back" in the new articles of war and in the regulations on military punishment of

67165

3 August 1808, issued on the king's birthday. With the king's consent these laws also referred to the introduction of universal conscription at some future time. Originally Scharnhorst had intended to create a national militia as an auxiliary to the regular army, but by the convention of September 1808 Prussia was forbidden to organize militias. Scharnhorst, however, had already discovered a way to make at least a beginning within the existing restrictions: the so-called Krümper system, which consisted in gradually training a larger number of men without officially raising the army's peacetime strength. Each company gave leave to three to five men, who were replaced by recruits; after being trained for one month these men were replaced in turn. In this way some 35,000 trained reservists were ready as early as the summer of 1811.

But farther than that the king was not yet willing to go. He did not sign the draft legislation on the introduction of conscription, submitted to him in 1809, and again in the following year. His own convictions led him to approve the preliminary steps on the way to universal military service. He personally called for the reduction of exemptions, the discharge of foreign soldiers, the abolition of corporal punishment. Did he consider the last, decisive step unnecessary? Was he concerned about the discontent of those groups that had once been exempt from service, especially the nobility? Was he made doubly cautious by the prospect of Napoleon's displeasure and suspicion, and perhaps by the fear that the regenerated army might someday be placed at the disposal of the French emperor? We do not know the answers. Here, as so often, a veil obscures the decisions of the taciturn ruler.

It is probably most accurate to suppose that Frederick William was guided by considerations of foreign policy. Of all internal reforms, universal military service would have had the greatest impact internationally. It would have been interpreted as a fanfare, a call for a new war, which was the goal of the reformers' planning and actions, but which the hesitant king wished to delay.

Let us now turn to the war itself. We cannot discuss it in breadth and depth, but we can interpret it by analyzing the high points of the struggle, the episodes in which material forces and individual energies reached extreme intensification. These climaxes are, for one, the major political issues that determined the course of events, and, secondly, the ideas and actions of the leading reformers as they contended with events and with the over-all situation.

CHAPTER 6

The Wars of Liberation

The struggle of the reformers against the international constellation that oppressed their country and their spirits bears similarities to their conflict with the traditions of the Frederician monarchy, which contradicted their vision of a new life and a new state. Here as there they gained great victories, but by no means all they wanted. Here, too, they often soared above reality and reached for the impossible. Even as they fought to free the state they did not pursue power politics pure and simple, and in the long run their policies had more momentous effects than could have been attained by a *Realpolitik* content with achieving the possible.

To understand these tensions and their resolution we must recognize the enormous discrepancy between Prussia's hopes and her power. A new sense of freedom and energy was spreading through society at the very time that the state had lost its independence. Prussia owed her continued existence solely to agreements concluded at the Peace of Tilsit and to the Franco-Russian alliance that resulted from the treaty. In 1807 the existence of the state in effect depended on Tsar Alexander. Consideration for Russia and the demands of his struggle with England induced Napoleon to allow Prussia to survive as a weak minor power, but under conditions that enabled him to crush her if she should impede his schemes or rebel against him. Occupation of Prussian territory, or at least of her major fortresses, for as long as possible, and an enormous indemnity were the thumbscrews he applied. Pressed and ringed in by Napoleon's vassals, the Confederation of the Rhine and the Grand Duchy of Warsaw, Frederick William placed his hopes in Alexander, But for the moment the tsar was busy gathering the fruits of his alliance with Napoleon, and all he offered Prussia was the advice to accept the inevitable. Later he was able to prevent the worst, French annexation of Silesia, and in this way the Franco-Russian alliance saved Prussia from declining still further, but the alliance also tied Prussia hand and foot and exhausted her economy.

Under these conditions Stein and Scharnhorst advised the king in 1807, and again in the following year, to put the state fully in Napoleon's hands, and offer him 30 or 40,000 Prussian soldiers for his wars to provide some relief from the terrible pressures. They made these proposals although they regarded Napoleon as the enemy of freedom. Their motives are difficult to interpret, but they must have hoped that such a link would enable Prussia to catch her breath and regain strength; perhaps they also hoped that Prussian victories would bring the state new military and political weight as well as territorial gains. When Scharnhorst once more advised closer ties with Napoleon in the summer of 1810, he said that as long as Prussia possessed "a degree of internal strength" such an association would not be all that dangerous and might lead to great advantages. But it would have been demonic to await the hour of revenge while embracing the enemy with hatred in one's heart, to recover strength by serving him. It would have meant seeking freedom by enslaving oneself. Such a policy suited forceful personalities, men who were confident of being free even in servitude, of remaining true to themselves, and of being able to break the chains when the time came. It was the policy of heroism that Kleist at that very time proclaimed in his *Hermannsschlacht,* the drama whose hero was both fox and lion. But could it be the policy of Prussian statesmen? The reformers forgot that they were not the state; it did not occur to them that by adopting their proposal and surrendering to the French system Prussia might undergo unintended internal and external changes, which would lead not to liberty but into still deeper servitude. It has been said that they prescribed poison to cure the desperate condition of the state. They did not doubt that they could tolerate the poison; but the state was organized differently from the body of a strong-willed man. Here, if anywhere, the individual soared far above and beyond the state, and the non-Prussian elements in the reformers' thinking were starkly revealed.

Soon their excessive strength reverted to the other extreme, but an extreme that suited them better. Napoleon rejected the Prussian offers of alliance, insisted on payment of the indemnity, and compelled agreement to the humiliating Convention of 8 September 1808. At the same time the Spanish struggle against French rule caused the first breach in Napoleon's authority, and Austria began preparations for a new war. The patriots' hopes rose. Suddenly they declared that an alliance with Napoleon would never prevent Prussia's destruction but merely postpone it. "Once in the Cyclop's Cave," Gneisenau said, "we can count only on the advantage of being devoured last." They argued that letting Austria fight alone and suffer defeat meant exposing Prussia to the certain fate of immediate disarmament as soon as the war ended. Every possible effort must now be made, Stein declared, every force must be put in motion. The reformers' determination is exemplified by their plans for a general insurrection in northern Germany, which would have led to a social revolution. Men who remained neutral or supported the enemy were to lose land and property. Gneisenau further demanded that territory that could not be held should be devastated, and women and children removed to inaccessible terrain. German princes whose troops joined the French should be dethroned and replaced by worthier rulers elected by the people. Titles of nobility that were not reconfirmed by bravery against the enemy should be abolished. And in the midst of these battles and upheavals Prussia, too, was to be rejuvenated and turned into a free and powerful constitutional state, "happy within its borders, respected and feared without." But could it be reconciled with Prussian *raison d'état* that Prussia at the same time was to declare her solemn intention not to acquire any German territory? "Only those German peoples that want to live with us under our laws will be accepted into our union." Revolutionary France had begun its war against the old Europe with similar ideals, and had concluded the fight in a very different vein. Much the same would have happened had Gneisenau's plans been adopted, but in the process Prussia would have ceased to be Prussia and become the center of new, unpredictable revolutionary configurations. Ultimately this more-than-Prussian statesman cherished a German, not a Prussian, ideal.

Stein was more firmly rooted than Gneisenau in the historical conditions of Europe, but at the time he, too, went beyond the limits of a leading minister and protector of the state's interests. His plans treated Prussia simply as a means of achieving the higher ends of the German nation. Stein demanded that all particularist ambitions should subside, that the rivalry between Austria and Prussia should end, that only one political symbol should be acknowledged: the combined colors—black, white, and yellow—of the two leading German states. Only his German patriotism could lead him to believe that without his monarch's knowledge and approval he had the right to pursue an independent policy, which held out the promise of assistance to Austria, promoted insurrection in northern Germany, and sought "to excite the spirit of the population, and bring it into ferment." The boldest move he considered was to offer Napoleon—at this moment!—Prussian assistance once more, to conclude the alliance, and as soon as Austria began the war to break it: "Is the Emperor Napoleon to be the only one allowed to substitute arbitrariness for justice, lies for truth?" With this plan his aroused energies broke through the barriers of his own ethical standards.

Frederick William could never have accepted such ruthless power politics. When one of Stein's letters promoting insurrection was intercepted by the French in the late summer of 1808, Stein's position was compromised so gravely that the king could have retained him only if he resolved on imminent war with France. The minister's Prussian enemies also raised their heads, above all the feudal party; but Hardenberg also warned the king and queen of the revolutionary, democratic implications of Steins plans. On 24 October 1808 Stein was dismissed. In a sense his fall was caused by a reaction of Prussian loyalties against his stormy German demands. Stein and his party did not shrink from the possibility that Prussia's uprising might lead to her downfall. The king, however, was willing to risk a war of liberation only if Russia as well as Austria would support him, giving him at least some assurance that Prussia would be preserved.

Consequently in 1809 Austria, not Prussia, began a struggle that potentially was a true national war for all of Germany. Since the experiences of 1805, a more vigorous spirit pervaded Austria; some of the leading men in government were adopting a broader outlook, and reformist tendencies, reminiscent of those in Prussia, surfaced in the army and administration. It is true that the energy and achievement of the Prussian program were not matched by the changes instituted by Count Philip Stadion's government and by Archduke Charles, the experienced commander-in-chief. When they appealed to the population to support the state's struggle against Napoleon they, like Frederick William and Hardenberg, feared that the popular forces could not be kept under control. Nevertheless in 1809 they risked organizing a genuine militia, a force that remained no mere creation of the authorities but also drew on popular enthusiasm and willingness to sacrifice. And when, in April 1809, Austria began the war on her own, without the support of allies, her self-interest compelled her to hope for uprisings in Germany and the force of nationalism in general. To her soldiers she declared: "Your German brothers, today still in the ranks of the enemy, await their deliverance," while Germany was told: "Accept the help we offer you. Join us in bringing about your salvation!"

Such appeals were still rejected in the Confederation of the Rhine. For the west-German states the French alliance was simply a matter of overriding self-interest, and by itself each state was undoubtedly defenseless against French pressure. As in Prussia, thorough administrative and economic reforms were carried out to fuse the state's haphazardly assembled territories into genuine political unity, but this goal was to be realized by administrative, not by national energies. And where, as for example in the former territories of the Teutonic Order along the Tauber river, the peasants took up arms on hearing of Austria's victory at Aspern, they expressed not a spirit of German nationalism but that traditional, particularist spirit that also characterized the uprising in the Tyrol under Andreas Hofer's heroic leadership.

A somewhat more modern, universally German spirit marked the isolated uprisings in northern Germany. Colonel Dörnberg in April 1809 and Colonel Emmerich two months later tried to overthrow the Kingdom of Westphalia, and Duke Frederick William of Brunswick led his small force on a daring march from Bohemia to the North Sea, aided by an aroused, hopeful populace.[1] Stein and the

1. Wilhelm von Dörnberg (1768–1850) and Andreas Emmerich (1735?–1809), Hessian officers. After Emmerich failed to turn the university town of Marburg into a center of insurrection he was captured and shot.

Prussian patriots counted on the spirit of the population; but conversely, in northwest and central Germany, men had to be able to rely on Prussia, or the uprising would be heroic but futile.

In 1809 calls for war came not only from the Prussian reformers, but from many groups in society. Without orders Major Schill led his hussar regiment against the French, and during the same April days even Count Goetzen, commander of the upper Silesian brigade, considered a surprise attack on the French garrison of Glogau.[2] Pressured by his advisors, by his generals, and—as he himself said— by his people, the king vacillated in May and again in July, only to return to a policy of neutrality as long as Russia did not join the war. "Your Majesty's system," his ministers defined it, "is to exorcise and calm as far as possible the storm threatening from France, to remain as independent from France as possible, and to move closer to Russia."

But even his ministers, among them Goltz, who in 1808, energetically opposed Stein's policy, now held different views, counseled war on the side of Austria, and found the king's attitude "unfortunate."[3] His own wife, Queen Louise, believed that one should not be dissuaded by the danger of annihilation. "At least we shall have the consolation," she wrote, "of ending our lives with honor, and what more can we ask for in a time such as ours?" In short, the contrast between the German policy of Stein and more narrowly Prussian policies was not absolute. Measured by normal standards, the king's policy of not risking the existence of his state would have been sound and realistic. But Napoleon constituted an anomalous, unpredictable power in the life of Prussia, a force that might continue to spare her but might also be preparing her sudden, ignominious end. Prussia exposed herself to this danger whether she remained passive or assumed a more active role. That constituted the weakness of Frederick William's policy and the strong point of the reformers' arguments. That, too, could induce better Prussians than Stein to think of joining Austria, even without the assurance of Russian support, before Prussia was totally isolated.

2. Ferdinand von Schill (1776-1809) led a poorly planned attempt to raise the Prussian countryside against the French. In a street battle in the town of Stralsund on the Baltic his force was destroyed and he was killed.

3. August Friedrich von der Goltz (1765-1832), Prussian diplomat, minister of foreign affairs.

The idea of a general uprising to prevent the possibility of a shameful end was bound to revive when the international situation changed completely in 1810 and 1811, and the Franco-Russian alliance collapsed. Russia would not permit herself to be used as a tool in the struggle against England, for which Napoleon was now preparing to exploit the resources of the entire continent. But because the two allies separated gradually and did not at once turn on each other, the situation of Prussia, the buffer between the two powers, became critical. The political base that had barely supported her since the Peace of Tilsit seemed to melt away without being immediately replaced by another, especially not by the only base that would have satisfied the king—an alliance of the three eastern powers, Prussia, Russia, and Austria. After her defeat in 1809 Austria became the ally of France, while Russia's intentions remained uncertain and unpromising. In the meantime Germany was inundated with troops, which Napoleon slowly moved to the east, and which would flood Prussia in the event of war. "Our greatest problem," Hardenberg wrote in August 1811, "is not knowing whether the break will come, and when." But even had this uncertainty been resolved, the options would scarcely have been less difficult. Those who courageously counseled war on Russia's side had to acknowledge not only the genius and greater strength of Napoleon, but also the tsar's well-known unreliability and weak character, and his plans of reconstituting Poland under a Russian prince, which would have seriously affected Prussia's position on the Baltic. On the other hand, as Hardenberg himself admitted, to join France would have led not only to greater dependence on Napoleon, but would not necessarily prevent destruction or truncation, as the recent downfall of the Dutch satellite kingdom had once again demonstrated.

Even Stein and Scharnhorst, as we know, had at times counseled complete submission to France, but only to break the deadlock, only as a last resort. The least gleam of hope reawakened the reformers' resolve. In 1811 it sufficed that the international balance was shifting, and that relations between the powers were again in flux. Surrender, Gneisenau now said, could only be the advice of a coward or traitor. "The emperor's power is not as terrible as it seems." Together with Scharnhorst and Boyen he reverted to the radical plans of 1808 for a popular uprising and guerrilla war in northern Germany. His plans and his recommendations to the king were, as he himself said, poetry of the subtlest kind—and such poetry is always both reality and illusion. Real above all was the moral force that informed these plans, but it was mixed with the illusion that the German people as a whole felt this force. The impression of Napoleon's boundless greed for conquest was realistic enough, but it, too, was partly illusory. The reformers' plans postulated a monolithic, primal force, driven by its instincts for power; but Napoleon was far from free—he was limited by international conditions and by his own political and dynastic considerations, by the "fluctuation of events" in which Hardenberg optimistically, but with sharp political instinct, placed his hopes. In the end, nothing was more realistic, even though based only on faith, than the assertion that the emperor's power was not as terrible as it seemed.

Such were the hopes and beliefs of the reformers, while at the same time they recognized that an uprising could destroy Prussia. "Let us meet the storm as men of honor," Boyen appealed to Hardenberg, "so that future generations will not wholly renounce this age." Even Boyen, the purest Prussian in the group, acknowledged values that towered above the preservation of the state at any cost. The spirit of the age as well as his own character spoke through him.

It will never be known whether the reformers' feverish mobilization measures in the summer of 1811 would have proved adequate for a war with France, and what might have happened to Prussia had they prevailed. Frederick William's acceptance of Napoleon's oppressive terms of alliance brought the crisis temporarily to an end and preserved the state during the invasion of Russia. The king's policy was eventually justified by external success; but it was justified only because the men who had dared more than he in 1808, 1809, and 1811 did not renounce Prussia. Without them the year 1813 would have taken a different turn for Prussia and Germany. The events of 1812 might easily have alienated the reformers from the state, and it was fortunate that in the end they were reconciled. In February 1812, when the king concluded the treaty that turned his state into a French satellite, some of the reformers left his service. They must have hoped that the separation would not be permanent, but who could know at the time for how long and how deeply the state would remain in servitude. Despair enveloped the men who left. One of them, Clausewitz, wrote in a memorandum placed "on the sacred altar of history": "I believe and confess that the shame of cowardly submission can never be erased; that this drop of poison in the blood of the people is transmitted to its progeny and will paralyze and undermine the strength of future generations." In the period of greatest tension, when Moscow had already burned, but Napoleon was still believed to be deep in Russia and Prussian troops were still fighting for him on the Baltic coast, Gneisenau bitterly exclaimed: "Poor Germany, tamed into slavery by your rulers, henceforth your best sons can fight only for an alien land." A curse lay on princes and the children of princes, he said during the same October days, and he repeated approvingly the word of Archduke Charles: "The world can be saved only by a man not born into a princely family." The revolutionary in Gneisenau emerged, condemning dynasties and tradition, and we might also say that his attitude exemplified Fichte's citizen of the world, who could settle wherever light and justice ruled. In November 1812 he placed his hopes in England, who, he said, should occupy parts of Germany, extend her constitution to the conquered territories, and integrate them into the British Empire, where "the peoples joined to Britain will experience well-being and happiness under a constitution of liberty." We can see that the national consciousness of even these men still remained different, more fluid than the firm nationalism of the later 19th century, which is patterned by the concept of absolute national independence and self-determination.

The situation in the fall of 1812 makes it understandable that such cosmopolitan currents again rose to the surface in these sons of the 18th century. At a time when Stein and Gneisenau were separated from their state and from German political forces, when they depended on England and Russia to carry on the struggle against Napoleon, they tended to evolve from representatives of a particular government into European statesmen. Gneisenau found a striking formulation for their new position: "The world is divided into those who, willingly or unwillingly, fight for Bonaparte's ambition, and those who oppose him. The basis of nationality seems less significant in this struggle than basic principles." Not only national, but also cosmopolitan and universal ideas now fought against Napoleon's universal monarchy, which contained its own cosmopolitan strain. Universal rule opposed universal freedom. To be sure, the concept of a free world encompassed the freedom of individual nations and states, but it was the superior, ultimate principle. As the champion of universal freedom, Stein could now demand that England, Austria, and Russia should reorganize Germany, and that Prussia must be forced to follow their lead. Just as he had once sought to achieve freedom by way of slavery, so he could now seek his nation's freedom through essentially un-national means. He wanted that part of Europe that remained free to build the great and powerful Germany, whose image, splendid as the Germany of the medieval emperors, filled his soul. What could individual German states mean to him? "At this juncture of great events and possibilities," he exclaimed, "I am entirely indifferent to dynastic interests. They are merely tools." Even Prussia mattered little. Let the state be dissolved, he said, and let Austria become master of Germany. "That is my wish, and it is good if it can be done." It might be objected that this was a momentary passionate outburst, but the outburst expressed profoundly-held beliefs. This single flash of lightning illuminates with new clarity that his loyalty was not to the Prussian state but to Germany, and beyond Germany to the realm of ethical freedom.

He was a statesman without a state; in his feelings as in his external condition, a citizen of that part of the world that was still free; a single, independent individual struggling against fate. The ideal of a free and vigorous life that recognized no superior authority except all-powerful fate, which the young Humboldt had once proclaimed, was uniquely and forcefully personified in this man. What Stein achieved at that time he achieved only through the personal influence he exerted on Tsar Alexander. But on the evidence we can assume that this influence changed the course of history. It appears to have been Stein who persuaded the tsar to carry the war beyond Russia's western border, to wage it not only as a national struggle but as a crusade for the liberation of Europe. The fate of Prussia and Germany depended on this decision; without it Prussia would have remained chained to Napoleon. Prussia's condition may seem humiliating: In 1807 the decision of a foreign power had been necessary to preserve Prussia at all, now again it was a foreign power that released Prussia's accumulated resources and energies. But if we know European history we will recall that during the Reformation the Protestant movement also depended on the decisions of the great powers. And even power does not rule exclusively. It was the combination of power and spirit, of international relations and the great individual, that led to Alexander's decision.

Not that Prussia awaited her fate in complete passivity. The king had entered into the French alliance because he believed Napoleon's fortune and genius to be invincible, but in his heart he was for Russia. As early as August he sent one of his adjutants, Major von Wrangel, to the commander of the Prussian auxiliary corps in Russia, with the secret advice that if the French were repelled and pursued beyond the Russian border, the Prussians should separate from the French and withdraw toward the East Prussian fortress of Graudenz. Mindful of this directive, but at the same time forced to make the ultimate decision on his own responsibility, the Prussian commander, Hans David von Yorck, on 30 December 1812 concluded the convention of Tauroggen, near the East Prussian border, with the Russians, by which the Prussian forces were temporarily neutralized. It was the first great signal, joyously received by the Prussian and German people, that the day of liberation was at hand. The effect was strengthened because the signal was given by a man whose character and personality invested his action with symbolic value and engaged the popular imagination. The courageous decision of the harsh, somber general came like a bolt of lightning from dark clouds.

But Yorck's decision did not yet mean that Prussia would change sides. It is true that since December 1812, by which time the destruction of the *Grande Armée* was obvious to everyone, Hardenberg was cautiously exploring the possibilities of an uprising against France. But in the first weeks of the new year the traditional and the new forces of the state once more struggled against each other. The new spirit called for national liberation, and pressed beyond the limits of exclusively Prussian interests for a general war waged by all Germans for Germany. The traditional outlook weighed the risks of such a conflict for the Prussian state. "I hear the cry: Germany, Germany!" one of its representatives, Ancillon, wrote to the king on 4 February, "let us recall that we are Prussians, first and foremost."[4] That was also the king's view, who now declared

4. Johann Peter von Ancillon (1767-1832), Protestant minister, later senior official in the Prussian foreign ministry.

he would act only in concert with Austria. Like the king, the Austrian government would have been content with a peace that somewhat restricted, but did not destroy, Napoleon's power. Fear of Russian superiority was replacing fear of the French, particularly fear of Alexander's plans to restore a Polish kingdom under Russian sovereignty. But it was scarcely possible to represent the Prussian point of view effectively without strengthening the army. Consequently reservists were called up to form new battalions; on 3 February the government issued a proclamation establishing detachments of *Jäger*, designed for the sons of upper and middle-class families, and on the 9th all exemptions from military service were lifted for the duration of the war. The enemy against whom these measures were directed was not yet identified, but the popular feelings that were being unleashed coincided with the intentions of the reformers and forced the king to change his policy. His generals were already making operational decisions on their own, and the people might rise up independently if the king hesitated much longer. On 23 February he finally decided to yield. On the 27th he concluded a military alliance with Russia; on 10 March the order of the Iron Cross was founded, and on the 17th the king issued a forceful and noble appeal "To my People," which was drafted by a member of the reform group, Councilor von Hippel.

And now the Prussian people really did take its place on the stage of history. Until 1813 it was still possible to doubt whether the "people," on whom the patriots counted in their plans for reform and uprising, did in fact exist, or whether it was merely a reflection, a postulate, of their ideals. The spring of 1813 removed all doubts. It is true that the characteristic division of the nation into a narrow stratum of educated society and a great majority of peasants, artisans, and subaltern officials was mirrored in the new military institutions: the volunteer *Jäger* detachments on the one hand, and the *Landwehr* on the other, a militia that according to the regulation of 17 March comprised all ablebodied men between the ages of 17 and 40 who were not drafted into the line regiments. But soon this dualism was overcome. In accord with Scharnhorst's ideas, the volunteer *Jäger* detachments provided the officers for the *Landwehr*, while the *Landwehr* became a true national institution by the very fact that the creation of its units was entrusted to local committees on which all classes were represented. What these committees achieved despite their few resources in the course of the next months proved that the old dualism between state and people had also been overcome. The bureaucratic, military state had not disappeared, and its discipline and authority remained indispensable, but the vigor with which it carried out the processes of mobilization were now felt to be the will of the nation. As Gneisenau had wished, the state now collaborated with those supreme elements of life, religion and poetry, which became the greatest of the "volunteers" that joined the nation's struggle. Ernst Moritz Arndt became both preacher and bard to his people. He preached of a God of Freedom, of a Lord of Rage and Power, and sang of the deepest feelings that filled the soldier. In the person of Theodor Körner, the young poet of Lützow's volunteers, poetry itself entered the field of battle, became a living force, and shared the death that every soldier faced, while Max von Schenckendorf's delicate and ardent lyrics linked the rising of the people to nationalistic elements of the romantic movement, and to dreams of past and future imperial splendor.[5]

Indeed, in all areas of thought and action the uprising brought past and future together. To gain a realistic impression of the war's specifically Prussian and Frederician features and of the military tradition it perpetuated, we can do no better than read the report of the British representative at Prussian headquarters, Sir Henry Lowe: "It is a general uprising of the people, but differs from that in Spain in that it has been firmly organized. The young men think it necessary to wear uniform and to drill before they are considered soldiers." Old-fashioned concepts of war are combined with ideas of the French Revolution in the *Landsturm* edict of 21 April 1813, which went beyond matters of uniform and drill to demand that the armed population wage a "war of self-defense, which hallows all methods." The edict's tone recalled the French Committee of Public Safety, and horrified not only the more extreme conservatives but also the bureaucracy. Since every conceivable popular emotion was being agitated, some impulses emerged that did not suit the class interests of the nobility. A later leader of Prussian conservatism, Leopold von Gerlach, could never forgive this feature of the age of liberation. "We forget," he remarked in 1850, "that the

---

5. Theodor Körner (1791–1813) and Max von Schenckendorf (1783–1817), patriotic poets. Adolf Ludwig von Lützow (1782–1834), Prussian general who led a free-corps in the Wars of Liberation.

enthusiasm of 1813 had a pronounced demagogic aftertaste." Even
if such feeble anxieties are discounted, however, the edict was not
workable. It went beyond the realm of the possible because the
people as a whole were neither as old-fashioned as were Spaniards,
Tyroleans, and Russians, nor as revolutionary as the French had
been in 1793. Consequently it was soon amended. But the edict,
together with its champions Gneisenau and Boyen, who passionately
resisted its weakening, demonstrates the soaring idealism and the
excess of energy, reaching for the impossible, without which even
feasible goals could not have been attained.

The total mobilization of Prussia's energies and resources, which
Stein had called for in 1808, now became reality. Scharnhorst and
Gneisenau would have been the natural leaders of the new army;
but readily though regretfully they made way for a more popular
figure, who incorporated the vitality and earthiness—if not the
highest ideals—of the regenerated state. To place a man like Geb-
hard von Blücher at the head of the army was to acquire an incomparable moral force. He inspired not only his own troops but affected
the course of the war as a whole. Again and again he was to tear
operations out of the doldrums and drive them forward. The
optimistic, vigorous old man, who as squire, hunter, and gambler
was accustomed to the Goddess of Fortune, now bound her to his
banner in a more serious cause. But he was not only the child of
nature; he had sound common sense, and was receptive to the more
liberal political views of his greater friends, Scharnhorst and
Gneisenau, who served under him as strategic advisor and chief
of staff.

Russia's policies and her destruction of the *Grande Armée*
initially enabled Prussia to enter the struggle, and Russia continued
to affect Prussia in favorable as well as unfavorable ways. In the new
alliance Prussia renounced the greater part of her former Polish
territories, which meant that compensation for her territorial losses
of 1807 would have to be found in Germany. As Russia expanded
westward she also pushed Prussia to the west, into Germany. It was
in keeping with this policy that the proclamation that the Russian
commander-in-chief Kutuzov issued at Kalisch on 25 March, at the
beginning of the Spring campaign, was addressed to the German
nation, in a sense turning the people against the princes still allied
to Napoleon, who were threatened with extinction "through the

power of public opinion and the force of righteous arms." Russia appealed to the national element in Prussia and Germany; but after her forces entered Germany her conduct of the war no longer expressed purely national Russian concerns, her initiative faltered and she immobilized the Prussian army, which had been placed under her supreme command. Scharnhorst's bold scheme of thrusting into northwest Germany and threatening the left flank of the advancing French was rejected; instead it was decided to await Napoleon in the plains before Leipzig. In that unfavorable defensive position the Allies were not yet a match for Napoleon's genius and superior numbers. In the battles of Grossgörschen on 2 May and Bautzen on 20 and 21 May, his stronger forces pushed the allied Russians and Prussians back to Silesia. Nevertheless, the course of the fighting convinced the defeated Prussians of their new powers. Observing his troops at Grossgörschen, Frederick William dropped his reins and called: "Whatever happens, it will not be another Auerstedt!" And at the end of the Spring campaign Gneisenau concluded: "The recent operations consisted of fighting of an intensity unequaled in history, so far as I know. Within four weeks we fought more than twenty sharp engagements and three days of battle. . . . But despite its steady retreat, the army has retained cohesion and its spirit is unbroken."

No doubt he once again overestimated Prussian power when he argued that the war could be continued even without the Russians, who were now withdrawing to Poland. But it must be repeated: Only the utmost resolution and self-confidence could compensate for the superiority that Napoleon still derived from unified leadership and greater numbers. Even so, the experiences of the Spring campaign induced the emperor to agree to a truce at the beginning of June, to give himself time to reinforce and train his young troops, and if possible to weaken the coalition by political maneuvers. Both sides wooed the Austrian government, which thus attained a decisive position. Like the timid advisors of the Prussian king, Francis I and Metternich were torn between fear of Russian and of French preponderance, until their cold realism convinced them that for the present the fight against Napoleon was more important than anything else. But it was scarcely realistic for them to believe that a great coalition could check Napoleon without having to destroy him. They steered toward a European balance of power, a system in which all national and revolutionary elements agitating the continent were laid to rest, and excessive ambition and power could be trimmed and pushed back. Austria's joining the coalition, which occurred on 12 August 1813, at the end of the truce, certainly brought about a highly desirable accretion of military strength, but her presence also caused a measure of political paralysis, which affected the conduct of operations.

A similar ally, who weakened as well as strengthened the coalition, was Crown Prince Bernadotte of Sweden. With his small Swedish auxiliary corps he hoped to help the coalition sufficiently to be rewarded with the crown of Norway. But he had to move cautiously; he could not afford to risk Sweden's resources and gamble with his own recent accession to power. Finally, behind and side by side with this continental coalition, comprising eastern and northern Europe, stood England, Napoleon's oldest and most stubborn opponent. A union of diverse interests and ideas, of continental and maritime powers, of legitimist-conservative and nationalist-liberal elements, of expansionist and of limiting forces, moved toward the decisive struggle.

To breathe in this friendly embrace, Prussia more than ever stood in need of the reformers' determination to seek the highest goals. When the truce ended she had raised more than 270,000 men, a figure that was increased in the course of the year to about 300,000, nearly 6 percent of the population. Not all these troops were of equal quality, and the numerous militia units in the field army still needed to be seasoned. But all in all it was a great achievement. "I don't know," Clausewitz said, "how far we could have come without Scharnhorst." Scharnhorst had died in Prague from the effects of a wound received at the battle of Grossgörschen. But in Gneisenau, Blücher's chief of staff and the guiding spirit of the field army, Prussia and the coalition possessed the "steel tip of the heavy iron wedge that will split the colossus"—to quote Clausewitz again.

Three armies were ranged against Napoleon: the Bohemian army, the Silesian army—made up of Prussian forces—and the Northern army. Each was to take the offensive but—so the Austrians and Bernadotte cautiously decided—each was to withdraw whenever it encountered Napoleon's main force. Of the three, the Silesian army was the smallest but the most aggressive. It evaded Napoleon's thrusts and fell on Macdonald to crush him at the battle of Katzbach on 26 August. With equal success Bernadotte's Northern army, in which the Prussian 3rd corps under Bülow and Boyen was the most active force, repelled Oudinot and Ney at Grossbeeren on 23 August and at Dennewitz on 6 September. Napoleon did push the main Allied army under the Austrian generalissimo Schwarzenberg back to Bohemia after defeating it at Dresden on 26 and 27 August. But the disasters suffered by Vandamme on 29 and 30 August at Kulm and Nollendorf where Kleist and Grolman distinguished themselves under the Russian commander Prince Eugene of Württemberg, robbed the emperor of the fruits of his victory. Still powerful but weakened by so many failures, Napoleon remained before Dresden. A true decision could only be achieved if at least two of the Allied armies combined forces. To bring this about Gneisenau chose the radical method of leading the Silesian army not toward Schwarzenberg in Bohemia, but through Lausitia and across the Elbe at Wartenberg, where Yorck forced the passage on 3 October, to a juncture with Bernadotte. Gneisenau's intention was to draw the Northern army with him, whether its commander agreed or not. But Bernadotte concurred, and crossed the Elbe in turn, while the Bohemian army began to advance on Leipzig from the south. Napoleon now threw himself against the united forces in the north, but failed to drive them back across the Elbe. Blücher and Gneisenau eluded him laterally to the west, with the result that the circle around Napoleon contracted so tightly that he was left only with the choice of withdrawing altogether or giving battle before Leipzig. Nothing like it had happened before. Napoleon had always sought out and attacked the enemy; now he was forced to stand and fight. Essentially it was Gneisenau's strategy that led to the unprecedented result.

It was also Blücher's army that caused the decisive turn on the first day of the battle of Leipzig. After Napoleon had fended off Schwarzenberg's advance on Wachau and Liebertwolkwitz south of the city on 18 October, and called on Marmont in the north to join the counterattack, he learned that Marmont's corps had been destroyed by Blücher's assault on Möckern. The French were now so tightly surrounded by far stronger forces that the outcome was no longer in doubt. Nevertheless Napoleon challenged fate once more. On the third day of the battle he managed to maintain his positions south and southwest of Leipzig, but again his forces north of the city were defeated, this time by the Northern army, led by Bülow's Prussians. The emperor was compelled to retreat. On the 19th, while his rearguard fought with desperate courage at the gates and in the streets of Leipzig, his main columns withdrew west along the highway to Weissenfels.

The "Battle of Nations" at Leipzig is one of those towering events in world history toward which all lines of development converge, and from which they radiate again in manifold rays. It had to happen, might be the conclusion of a view of history that surveys the major forces in the lives of peoples and of states. More careful reflection would add that it could only have happened because these general forces also expressed the most personal feelings and actions of individual men. States, nations, and men excelled on both sides at the battle of Leipzig. The one idea of destroying Europe's oppressor united the dim feelings of the common soldier, the balanced calculations of the statesman, and the ideals of those outstanding individuals, the supreme representatives of the age of liberation, in whom this study is especially interested. For these men the overthrow of Napoleon was the immediate goal of all their efforts, and at the same time a step toward still greater heights— reality and symbol had come together, the finite and the infinite. When these coincide, men may be filled with the sense of supreme happiness that Stein and Gneisenau now experienced. A further intensification was not possible; from here on their road still ran along the heights, but gradually it descended. Their new goals aroused new opposition, which they were unable to overcome. The further expansion of their reforms into a vital nation-state, which met the needs of the individual as well as of the community, was denied them because the traditional forces with which they had jointly fought against the common enemy now turned against them.

Austria became the leader of these traditional forces, of legitimist, conservative Europe. Now that France had been driven back to western Europe, Emperor Francis and Metternich wanted to push Russia and Prussia back to the east. They did not want Russia to acquire Poland, nor Prussia Saxony, whose ruler had remained loyal to Napoleon and might therefore have been subjected to the judgment threatened by the Declaration of Kalisch. To prevent other dangerous national developments in Germany and to reward the king of Bavaria for renouncing the French alliance, Austria had already acknowledged his continuing sovereignty. She continued the struggle against Napoleon, but with reduced military energies that resulted from her system of political balance. Her task was eased by Alexander's vacillating and by Frederick William's chronic hesitation. From their headquarters in Frankfurt the Allies in December 1813 offered Napoleon the so-called natural borders of France, which included the left bank of the Rhine. Their armies did not enter France until the beginning of the new year. With further victories they planned to increase their demands, but still did not intend to destroy the root of the problem, the emperor's reign in France. Negotiations with Napoleon continued on French soil, at the Congress of Chatillon from 5 February to 18 March, although their three-fold superiority might have led the Allies to risk the attempt to crush him. Once more Napoleon had the opportunity of employing his genius and the advantages of unified command to magnificent effect. At Brienne on 29 January and at Champaubert and Etoges-sur-Marne from 10 to 14 February he struck hard at Blücher's army, which again had advanced most rapidly. Between these setbacks, Blücher supported by the main army fought the successful defensive battle of La Rothière on 1 February; but he could not prevent Napoleon from exploiting his victories on the Marne by again attacking Schwarzenberg on 18 February at Montereau and forcing the Austrians to give ground.

Schwarzenberg, inhibited by his government's policies and intimidated by the defeat, already thought of further retreat when the extremists in Blücher's headquarters again pushed matters forward. Grolman worked out a plan and managed to have it approved that detached Blücher from the main army and had him march north to combine with a Russian corps under Wintzingerode and with Bülow, who had moved south from Holland, so that they could continue the offensive independently from the main army. Napoleon hurried after them but on 9 and 10 March was repulsed before the steep heights of Laon, a battle which for once brought together the most distinguished of Prussia's generals—Blücher, Gneisenau, Kleist, Yorck, Bülow, Grolman, Boyen. Should they exploit their victory by fully committing their reserves? Even in the Prussian camp some argued that now that Napoleon's collapse was only a matter of time Prussia ought to preserve her armies to give the state greater weight in the peace negotiations. It was indeed difficult to think that the emperor could still survive. Schwarzenberg had resumed his advance, won an engagement at Bar-sur-Aube on 27 February, and then had defeated Napoleon himself on Arcis-sur-Aube on 20 and 21 March. Napoleon played a last, desperate card by moving the small army that remained to him to the rear of his enemies and threatening their lines of communication. But after overcoming their first shock, the Allies continued to advance on Paris. A few final encounters with Marmont and Mortier at La Fère Champenoise on 25 March and before Paris on 30 March, and the heights of Montmartre were reached. As Gneisenau stood there, surveying the captured capital of the enemy, now conclusively defeated, an eyewitness tells us that the glory of victory radiated from his face.

*   *   *

The first Peace of Paris, concluded on 30 March, exiled Napoleon, restored the Bourbons, and returned the Rhineland to Germany, though without Alsace and Saarbrücken. Slowly but relentlessly the European coalition completed its work. Gneisenau and his associates had been the yeast in the coalition's strategy, but without the hundreds of thousands of Allied troops they could never have reached their goal. Prussia's situation was analogous. She was now internally strong; in proportion to her size she had achieved far more than her two eastern allies. But as the smallest of the three she remained politically dependent on them. Her relative and her absolute power were not in accord. She could not pursue a purely Prussian policy in foreign affairs, as Frederick had managed to do, because by herself she was too weak, and she could not choose her allies. The same powers that helped her regain her independence now held her back. Enveloped in their system, she was compelled to accept the territorial settlement arranged in the great congress that convened in Vienna. Nevertheless, her achievements in the war and the treaties she had concluded gave her hope that she would be reasonably compensated for her losses of 1807.

The hopes of the German nation were less promising. The Agreement of Ried, which guaranteed independence to Bavaria, also benefited the other medium-sized states and destroyed any possibility of a unified, effective federal structure. The reformers, whose hopes had always embraced Germany as well as Prussia, had to resign themselves to that fact. "Designing a good German constitution, which would eventually be accepted, strikes me as impossible," Gneisenau wrote to Hardenberg on 15 May. "Consequently I think we should limit ourselves to Prussia's interests, whose protection is our first concern." He did not permanently renounce a closer union of Prussia with Germany, but now he wanted to pave the way to this union through the attraction exerted by Prussia's ethical ideals, the "liberality of her principles." Prussia was to become a model state, "splendid in the three areas that alone enable a people to become great: military glory, a constitution and the rule of law, and the flowering of the arts and sciences."

Even this more limited task constituted a major challenge, and Gneisenau may have underestimated its difficulty if he believed that under current conditions, purely on her own, Prussia could accomplish the task in grand style. As we have seen, a state's foreign and domestic affairs are so closely related that one area cannot be nurtured intensively while the other is left fallow. The international constellation which Prussia now joined, the Holy Alliance with its conservative spirit, could not remain without influence on the country's domestic affairs, the more so since it found natural allies in the nobility and among conservative bureaucrats, who had suspiciously watched the unfolding of a freer national life. Most ministers who now served under Hardenberg belonged to this faction: Kaspar von Schuckmann at the head of the important ministry of the interior; Prince Wittgenstein, the scheming and distrustful minister of police; and Friedrich von Kircheisen, the minister of justice. The only vigorous reformer in the ministry since June 1814 was Boyen, who as Scharnhorst's successor now was officially made minister of war. Such was the heterogeneous character that Hardenberg, always the eclectic, gave to the cabinet charged with conducting the work of reconstruction and development. At first, to be sure, the purifying effect of the Wars of Liberation suppressed the partisan conflicts that were to permeate the next phase of Prussian history, and Boyen grasped the opportunity to give permanence to the greatest military-political idea of the reform era, that of universal conscription, which so far had been introduced only for the duration of the war. The law of 3 September 1814 established the general obligation of three years' active service, followed by two years in the reserves. Men who had passed through army and reserve, as well as those who for budgetary reasons had not been conscripted, served in the militia, the *Landwehr,* and during crises all other men who could bear arms were united in the *Landsturm.* The educated classes were conscripted in a manner that appealed both to their idealism and their self-interest. After one year in the regular army, the sons of well-to-do and educated families were given first claim on officer commissions in the *Landwehr.* In extension of Scharnhorst's original plans, a national military organization of impressive unity, force, and flexibility was created, indeed, one is tempted to say, was improvised—Boyen brought it about so quickly and easily. The Prussian system became the most significant model for modern military institutions in general, and, it has been said, was adopted throughout the world. But before this could happen the new institutions passed through severe crises. Elements of the old Frederician manner, especially the officers' aristocratic caste spirit, re-emerged and opposed the freer, middleclass forms of the militia. Some of Boyen's innovations lacked enough military strictness and efficiency to survive the conflict. He had relied on the strength of individual character and on patriotic sentiment at the expense of drill and experience. That is, he invested the new institutions with too many of those precious qualities that the reformers had borrowed from the treasures of German culture and offered to the state—with more, at any rate, than this innately rigid state could accept.

But in 1814 Boyen owed his new political power to those qualities. If the king and Hardenberg were at last prepared to accept Boyen's military legislation it was largely because at the coming Congress of Vienna they intended to impress Europe with a Prussia secure in the armor of universal conscription. Once again the links between domestic and foreign policy, between reform and power, are revealed. In the crises of 1809 and 1810, when the king subordinated power to the mere need for survival, he rejected compulsory military service. Now that conscription had helped revive Prussia's power in the Wars of Liberation he may have shared Boyen's hope that making conscription permanent would lend emphasis to Prussian aims at the congress.

These aims were twofold. For one they sought the acquisition of Saxony, which would link and consolidate Prussia's fragmented territories in a highly desirable way. Frederick the Great had toyed with the same idea. If Prussian diplomats and generals sought Saxony as the major compensation for the former Polish provinces, now claimed by Russia, they not only wanted to round off the state advantageously and increase its population, but by incorporating this highly developed German population they hoped to infuse Prussia with new blood to speed its maturity into nationhood. The heterogeneous Prussian and Saxon territories could be fused, Boyen believed, "through an appropriate constitution. . . . a magnificent nation might then arise." Eighteenth-century ideas survived in his belief that a nation could be created by wise legislation, that nationhood could be imposed as liberty had been imposed. What was more, the new allegiance was to be forced on a people most of whom were passionately loyal to the traditional dynasty. But we must not forget that the concept of nation was only developing. It was still a vague force in which old and new mingled; an idea not yet formed, but one capable of being shaped and one that could easily stimulate the creativity of a political idealist.

In 1815 these wishes were only partly fulfilled. The Saxon issue, closely tied to the Russian and Polish question, became a European issue, which at the beginning of the year even threatened to errupt in war. At the Congress of Vienna, Prussia and Russia were opposed by Austria, which neither wished to see Poland in Russian hands nor Saxony part of Prussia. Austria was supported by Bourbon France, whose representative Talleyrand wanted to check Prussia's rising power, and by England, fearful of Russian expansion. On 3 January 1815 the three powers concluded a secret military agreement; at the same time Gneisenau, Grolman, and Boyen drafted plans for a national German war over Saxony, in which the population would be unleashed against those princes who refused to support the struggle. Both Prussia's and Germany's future would have been decided by such a war. Prussia would have been driven still farther into the national German sphere, and the problem of the German nation—the relationship between Prussian and German nationhood—would have been resolved by the sword. But the time for that radical decision had not yet arrived. Prussia was not yet strong enough, and her alliance with Russia was not yet sufficiently solid for such a solution. While Russia was able to implement her

Polish plans, Frederick William and Hardenberg accepted a settlement that left the core of Saxony to its dynasty and gave Prussia only the northern part of that country. Instead she received more Rhenish territories than she had demanded, and thus the mission of defending Germany's western frontier against France. In the long run this solution did probably more for Prussian penetration of Germany than the acquisition of the entire Saxon kingdom would have done. Strengthened and consolidated by the incorporation of all Saxony, Prussia would have been satiated, and might have grown in a more specifically Prussian rather than German direction. By being drawn farther west into Germany than she liked, Prussia was divided into two separate land masses, but she was also woven more firmly and intimately into the texture of the whole German nation. Her new geographic fragmentation between east and west was as beneficial to 19th-century Prussia, approaching her German mission, as it had been to the old territorial, military state.

At the time, as Gneisenau recognized, Prussia's future mission had to be relegated to second place. But that Prussia had this mission was already sensed and gave rise to the second aim she pursued at the Congress of Vienna. As we have seen, even Boyen, the most rigorous Prussian among the reformers, could not strictly separate Prussian and German nationality. The two forces mingled in the convictions of the men who had liberated the country from Napoleon. Their union, albeit inarticulate, had inspired the Prussian uprising, and had awakened the thought in ambitious men—in the liberal Boyen no less than in the neo-feudal Junker Marwitz— that Prussia must become the dominant force in Germany, at least north of the Main river. But this political and military sense of power to which the future belonged, was opposed by another national idea, deeply rooted in the character of the age. If Boyen and Marwitz looked from Prussia to Germany, Stein conversely looked from Germany to Prussia, with Prussia's obligations toward Germany but not her claims to Germany in mind. Stein's national ideal was ethical rather than political in character. Of course he hoped that a union of German states would become a true political power, but the purpose of this power was above all to guard the nation's free and moral existence against the despotism of princes and bureaucrats and against the return of French tyranny. In that way a strong Germany would also serve European society and the community of European states, and therefore Stein was even prepared to have Germany's political existence guaranteed by the other major powers that had fought against France. That meant allowing foreign governments to interfere in German affairs, and endangered the absolute autonomy of his own nation. Stein, of course, hoped that the great powers would not abuse their role, but would cooperate to protect the peace and freedom of Europe. Once again we see his national ideal expand into a universal concept and a trace of 18th-century cosmopolitanism appear in his thought.

But a politically viable organization could not be constructed from these ideals, and inevitably Stein's projects, which sought to do the impossible, assumed strange forms. He wanted to give the German imperial crown to Austria rather than to Prussia, although—or, in his view, precisely because—Austria was not as completely German as was Prussia. The imperial dignity would bind Austria to Germany, while Prussia, he said in 1813, should be neither directly subordinated to Austria nor alienated from Germany—an impossibly utopian attempt to reconcile the irreconcilable, but understandable once again on the basis that ethical ideals, not power egotism, were to guide political life.

Stein's concepts did not guide the Prussian representatives at the Congress of Vienna. Hardenberg and Humboldt guarded Prussia's interests more firmly than he did; but they, too, had an optimistic faith in the ability of Austria and Prussia to work together harmoniously in Germany. They hoped to satisfy both Germany's national needs and the special interests of the two major German powers. Only boldness and force could resolve these ambiguities, and since Prussia, as we saw, felt too weak to go to war, nothing remained but to accept the loose German confederation proposed by Austria and the medium-sized states. The outcome was the threadbare contrivance of the German Federal Act of 8 June 1815, whose basic articles became part of the final document of the Congress, and thus were guaranteed by the other signatories. The settlement kept the two strongest German states within the new German political framework. The whole was oriented toward their peaceful cooperation, which meant that the new confederation incorporated all the fragile and questionable features of Stein's projects, while their vital elements—the demand for internal freedom and for a strong defensive capability against external enemies—were allowed to atrophy.

In this manner the great movement that tried to bind the Prussian state intellectually and politically to the German nation was blocked by the great powers, which opposed a further increase in Prussian strength, and by Germany's own particularist interests, which resisted the reduction of their political autonomy. But the movement was not only inhibited from the outside; as we saw, it had not yet matured, it lacked clarity, it still contained too much that was unrelated to the state and went beyond the state, too much personal idealism, whose riches were the reformers' strength, whose excess their weakness.

External events seemed to throw everything into flux once more when Napoleon returned to France from Elba, and Europe again faced the task of defeating him. In the shock and uncertainty of the moment, German patriots, even in the former Confederation of the Rhine, turned to Prussia, whose hegemony in Germany now seemed to offer the best hope for Germany's independence and future. Even Hardenberg entered into communication with these groups and persuaded the king to promise the Prussian people a constitution and a representative assembly. But the same international crisis that elicited these hopes and the moves toward more liberal, national policies also tied Prussia more firmly to the other powers and to their common mission of defeating Napoleon. Foreign developments and her own interests forced her to rejoin the general European coalition against the threat to the balance of power, and she lost the chance of being rewarded for her cooperation by receiving concessions in Germany.

Once more the Prussians under Blücher marched to Belgium, where they joined the English forces under Wellington to fight for the cause of Europe, as they had a century before with Marlborough. Once more they proved their incomparable qualities by recovering from the defeat at Ligny on 16 June and coming to Wellington's assistance, a maneuver that decided Napoleon's defeat. Once again Gneisenau showed himself a great commander by his march on Belle Alliance and later by the pursuit of the defeated enemy, disregarding exhaustion of man and beast to complete the work of destruction. And the same energies that had triumphed in battle

[127

now rushed into the political arena. The headquarters of the Prussian army became the source of the most stringent demands that the powers presented to France. In Gneisenau's and Boyen's view, the cession of Alsace and Lorraine would make territorial exchanges possible among the German states, which would lead to a restructuring of Germany and the growth of Prussian power. But they encountered the united resistance of their allies, and their impassioned advocacy aroused suspicion and anxiety not only of foreign diplomats but among Prussians as well. They were again regarded as Jacobins, revolutionaries who appealed to popular forces and endangered legitimacy and the status quo. Over their heads the Second Peace of Paris was concluded, which imposed only a few additional sacrifices on France. Saarbrücken now became Prussian.

*   *   *

In this manner the Age of Liberation came to an end. Its results were unsatisfactory if aims and achievement are compared. The reform movement was also marked by an internal split: its leaders were individualists who could not fully harmonize their own ideals and demands with those of the state. We stressed this cleft and dissonance, not only to reject trivial, patriotic legends, but because the peculiar greatness of the reformers is founded on this lack of harmony. It is inspiring to see these demanding and ambitious men attempt not only the possible but also the impossible, and soar far above political realities. In their upward flight they did not ask whether they would crash, and thus they awake in those who understand them a sense of the infinite, which enables us to bear the finite. Their personalities and actions also infused this sense into the state and the nation, and gave them ideals that can never be fully realized but are always effective. If in the first decade of the twentieth century men can regard the state as more than a cold and oppressive force, and the nation as more than a primitive racial concept, if both seem to offer spiritual clarity and warmth, an atmosphere in which the free individual can breathe, then in Germany it is due largely to the Prussian reformers.

Index of Names

[129